Song of a Christian Sufi

A Spiritual Memoir

SONG OF A CHRISTIAN SUFI

A Spiritual Memoir

MARIETTA BAHRI DELLA PENNA

ANAMCHARA
BOOKS

Song of a Christian Sufi:
A Spiritual Memoir

Anamchara Books
Vestal, NY 13850
www.anamcharabooks.com

9 8 7 6 5 4 3 2

Paperback ISBN: 978-1-937211-76-9
ebook ISBN: 978-1-937211-77-6

Library of Congress Control Number: 2014942345

Author: Marietta Bahri Della Penna

Cover design by Ellyn Sanna.
Interior design by Camden Flath.

All quotations from Rumi, Hafiz, and other mystic writers, as well as all scripture quotations, unless otherwise indicated, are the publisher's own versions.

Image credits: Elena Ray Microstock Library © Elena Ray; © S-E-R-G-O, Dreamstime.com.

For my Bill,
with love and gratitude
for filling each day
with new beginnings.

I call to remembrance my song . . .
I commune with mine own heart,
and my spirit makes diligent search.
Psalm 77:6 KJV

I

Ponder the starting point of your life. . . .
Through the song of your being
runs the Melody of Life.
Rumi

"Now I lay me down to sleep." That prayer was my first connection to the concept of God. "I pray the Lord my soul to keep. If I should die before I wake, I pray the Lord my soul to take."

The words terrified me. They triggered all sorts of questions in my child's mind: What if I really died before I woke? The prayer implied that such an event was altogether too likely. How did you die? What would it feel like? What was a soul? Where would I be when I died? These may have been the first intellectual inklings of theology I experienced, but they were chilly thoughts that brought me no comfort.

I can't remember who taught me to repeat this prayer at bedtime, whether it was my mother or father. Neither of my parents were churchgoers, although they were married in church and came from a long line of Roman

Catholics. My mother never tired of saying that people who went to Mass were hypocrites because afterward they gossiped on their way out of church. My father didn't particularly care about religion one way or another—except for those occasions when he was inclined to invoke God's authority to prove himself right.

But my parents' families came from Italy, where religion and culture were stubbornly woven together, and when I was growing up, Italian families living in the Bronx were not that far from the Old Country. The Church's calendar scheduled our family gatherings. We celebrated our name days—the sacred days of the saints after whom we were named—like birthdays. And when the Church's holy days came around, we feasted. The Church's annual cycle offered us—and all good Catholics—occasions to eat, drink, and be merry.

In my child's mind, chief of all holy days was Christmas. Our Christmas Eve dinners were seven courses of various fish, a reminder of the days when good Catholics abstained from eating meat on Christmas Eve; instead of meat, we ate baccalà (dried cod), calamari, scallops, whiting, scungilli (sea snails), clams, and even lobster. All that was a mere appetizer, though, compared to what we would eat on Christmas Day.

On Christmas Eve we attended Midnight Mass, where the boys' choir sang in Latin, their soprano voices transporting us to a place where the birth of Christ was not only history but a living reality. Once home again, we came back down to earth. Cocoa awaited us, and so did the Christmas tree, newly decorated. Huge red, green, gold, and silver balls hung from the boughs, and colored lights and silver tinsel twinkled like fairy fires amid the evergreen. We Italians got the gifts out of the way on Christmas Eve; we knew we needed to leave plenty of time for the holiday's most important event—Christmas dinner.

The feast began on Christmas Day with trays of antipasto. After that, we sat down to bowls of clear-broth soup, followed by lasagna. Then came the main course: roast beef. Served with it were artichokes, eggplant parmigiana, stuffed mushrooms, roasted potatoes, roasted peppers, fried asparagus, Italian bread, and to lighten us up, salad. My parents, grandparents, aunts, and uncles drank glasses of white and red wines with the food. Periodically, we'd all swallow one of the jarred cherries that had been marinating in hard liquor for years. The cherries were meant to settle our stomachs; the alcohol was so strong, it burned up any bits of undigested food. But that still wasn't enough. Dessert was every type of cookie that had ever been made back in the Old Country, as well as fruit pies, dates, pomegranates, figs, and roasted nuts.

By the time the grownups were sipping tiny cups of demitasse and Sambuca, the day was almost over. Sitting around the table—eating, drinking, and talking (with or without shouting)—had taken between five and seven hours. Fiery arguments might have occasionally interrupted those hours, but there was more laughter than anger; it was Christmas Day, after all, and petty irritations could wait for another time.

Easter was a bit more subdued than Christmas, perhaps because we were all feeling rather solemn after Holy Week, not to mention the six weeks of Lent before that. Nevertheless, it was a joyful time. We'd go to church on Easter morning dressed in our new pastel dresses and our best suits, we girls wearing multicolored bonnets (with or without flowers), while the boys' ties were knotted and straight. On the way home, I would admire my feet as they tapped along the sidewalk in their new patent-leather shoes.

Once inside our building, the hallway would be rich with the scent of roasting lamb and onions. My grandmother and aunts were already inside the apartment, helping my mother prepare for another day of feasting.

This time when we sat down at the table, my mother would bring out ravioli or manicotti (because no meal could possibly be complete without pasta), followed by baby lamb mixed with scrambled eggs, and then the large roasted lamb. We were remembering Christ, the Lamb of God, but none of us felt the least compunction at stuffing our mouths with the savory meat. Our faith was a very *fleshy* one.

Dessert consisted of candied baked bread with hard-boiled eggs buried in the dough. While the grownups drank their wine, we children had chocolate bunnies, colored eggs, and jellybeans, sweet symbols of the Resurrection and the new life of Christ.

My extended family was devout, but in an odd sort of way. My grandmother, mother, and aunts didn't attend church except for weddings, funerals, and masses for dead relatives. When they did, on occasion, visit a church, they would cry, kiss the crucifix, pray the rosary—and call upon God to deliver them from each other.

And so faith was the background of my life, but it was an unspoken faith, a faith expressed more deeply through food than through prayer or Scripture reading. Culture, religion, and family were so tightly intertwined that none of us could have picked apart the strand even had we tried—but we did not talk about theology.

When I was old enough, my parents sent me to a Catholic school, but they were concerned about status rather than religion. Public schools were for the ordinary masses, they reasoned; the kids there were undisciplined, everyone knew, and the hallways were filled with crime, while the academics were inferior. On the other hand, Catholic school students wore tidy uniforms, and they were respectful and better educated. Like many immigrant Italians, my parents were intent on climbing the proverbial ladder of success. Sending their child to a Catholic school was an important rung on that ladder.

They never guessed that when I entered school, I was embarking on a life of spiritual searching, a quest that would continue long after they were dead and gone. My parents simply didn't think like that. Their lives had taught them to focus on other things.

✳✳✳

My father was thirteen years old, penniless, and unable to speak English, when he set foot on Ellis Island. His parents and siblings had arrived seven years earlier, but as the eldest son, he had been left behind with his grandparents to help tend the family farm. What must have it been like for him, only a young child, to have his parents leave him like that? The seven years between six and thirteen are long ones; by the time his mother and father finally sent for him, his parents and siblings must have been a dim memory in his mind.

His father met him at the boat and then drove him to the family home in South Philadelphia, one of those four-story attached houses with white marble steps leading to the front door. (I heard the story countless times of my youngest aunt who as a teenager had to get on her hands and knees and scrub, scrub, scrub those marble steps till they mirrored the sun. Her example was supposed to inspire me to similar heights of goodness, strength, and perseverance.)

On the top floor of the building was an entire apartment, where an aunt and her husband lived; my grandfather used the cellar for making wine; and the remaining two floors were the family's living quarters. At the rear of the house was a kitchen big enough to dance the polka on its tile floor. I remember standing there in the doorway, watching my mother with my paternal grandmother and aunts laboring over the pots and pans, beads of sweat rolling off their faces and down their necks. I vowed I'd never grow up to be like them; I already was quite certain there was more to life than cooking.

In the dining room stood a huge mahogany table. Perhaps I remember it so clearly because during each of my childhood visits to my grandparents, my father lifted me up onto the table's long, shiny surface and commanded that I sing: "A tiskit, a taskit, a green and yellow basket." Ella Fitzgerald had made the song famous, but my parents gave the credit to that cute little white girl, Shirley Temple. By the time I was three years old, I not only had the voice but also the curls to match Shirley's, so the scene was right out of one of her movies. I would have preferred to run away and hide rather than be the center of attention—but my father's will was stronger than mine. Once I began singing, I could concentrate on the words and gestures, though, and as always, singing banished my fears. In those days, whenever I sang, I dimly sensed a mysterious, loving Someone who sang with me, a Voice that harmonized with my own.

But the days when I would sing on the dining room table for a room full of relatives were still years in the future when my father arrived that day from Italy. The family had kept the news of his coming a secret from my grandmother, so as the door of her sitting room swung open, she had no idea that her firstborn was about to enter. When she saw him, she cried, "Alessandro! Alessandro!" and flung herself into his arms.

Years later, my father told this story over and over. The memory was clearly precious to him, a moment to which he mentally returned again and again. I wonder now if this was the only time he truly knew his mother loved him.

Meanwhile, my grandfather was only concerned with the practical implications of his son's homecoming. He wanted his eldest son to learn a skill to help support the family; he suggested tailoring, a lucrative and respectable trade among Italians.

But my father had other ideas. During his years in Italy, separated from his parents, he had come to see an education as the greatest value life could offer. Education, he believed, would bring him security and independence. Although he dabbled in tailoring to please his father, he had already made up his mind about his goals. At the age of thirteen he entered grade school and worked his way through as quickly and efficiently as possible. From there, he somehow dispensed with high school altogether and pushed his way directly into the Drexel Institute of Technology. He graduated with an engineering degree and went to work for the City of New York.

Throughout my lifetime, I'd often hear my father bemoan the fact that he wasn't in private industry, where he could have made more money. But the fear of another Great Depression hung over everyone in the days when my father was entering the working world. He opted for job security over a high salary.

***

My mother had even fewer options in life than my father had, although she had been born in this country and had attended school from the time she was small. As a woman, not many careers were open to her. After she finished the eighth grade, she went to a trade school, where she learned to sew. She wanted to become a bookkeeper or an accountant, but these careers were out of the question. They required more education, and education took money.

My mother was the second child of four girls, with the third daughter arriving just ten months after my mother was born. Since my grandmother could no longer nurse her older baby, she put coffee in a bottle and gave that to her ten-month-old daughter instead. Perhaps those early doses of caffeine were what made my mother the driven woman she became. She grew up to be talented and intelligent, more so than her sisters, yet she always seemed to feel she needed to prove something to the world. She felt as though she had been invisible to her mother.

As a child, I learned that my mother didn't like to talk about her childhood or her family. If I asked questions, she'd become annoyed, so I stopped asking. But she did like to tell me about the injustices she had suffered at dressmaking school and in her workplace.

The teachers in her school, she told me, had been merciless. If any of the girls made a mistake, the teachers forced them to rip apart everything they had sewn and begin again. The students had only a quick half-hour for lunch, and no breaks during grueling ten-hour days, with little heat in the winter and one small fan in the summer.

Once the girls graduated, their workplace wasn't any better. Seamstresses worked long hours, the pay was poor, and the conditions terrible, at least until the Ladies Garment Workers' Union was formed. To make matters worse, the work was seasonal, which meant my mother couldn't earn anything during much of the year. She had no other professional opportunities, though, for few jobs were open to women. Nevertheless, she was expected to help support her family until she married.

My mother was fiercely ambitious. As a woman in the 1930s, '40s, and '50s, she had little scope to satisfy her own ambitions, however, and so, once she had children, she transferred them to my brother Nicky and me. She was relentless in her demands that we be as competitive and determined as she was.

For me, that translated into "bettering myself" socially. "Tell me who you go with and I'll tell you what you are," was one of my mother's favorite statements, one I heard countless times as I grew up. The friends I chose were never good enough for her. They didn't speak well enough, didn't come from good enough families; they didn't wear the right clothes. Over and over, I disappointed my mother.

***

But those demands on my social life came later. When I was very young, before I went to school, I was allowed to play with children who lived on the block, especially Sara. Her mother, Ann, and my mother had been childhood friends, so my mother considered Sara a suitable playmate for me. Besides, her family was "our kind of Italians"—they had come from the "right" section of Italy, wore finer clothes, and were better educated than some Italian immigrants.

One day in early spring, Ann took Sara and me on a small outing. Pushing our doll carriages and chattering "grownup talk" to each other, Sara and I followed Ann to the park down the street. There, Ann found a bench close to a grassy spot, and Sara and I spread out a picnic for our dolls. As we played, I noticed that Ann occasionally looked up from her knitting to smile at us. In my five-year-old head, I soberly considered this action of hers—and then reached the conclusion that Ann smiled at us like that because she was a good mother. Immediately on the heels of this deduction came another realization: I loved Ann. Happiness and a sense of freedom enclosed me, like a pair of warm arms. I wanted the afternoon to last forever.

All too soon, though, it was time to leave. Ann and Sara walked back with me to my apartment building, and I climbed up the stairs to the third floor. Below me, I knew Ann and Sara were waiting in the lobby; when I reached our apartment door, I called down the stairwell to let them know I had safely arrived. Ann—the good mother—could leave now and go home.

I sighed and went inside.

I found my mother in the kitchen. She turned from the sink and glared at me, but neither of us said a word for a long moment. I knew she was angry, though I could not imagine why. All I could do was stare back at her, frozen by her gaze. The rest of the world disappeared from my awareness, leaving nothing but her black, black eyes. They seemed to me like deep inkblots dropped onto the kitchen's shiny whiteness. I felt I might fall into them and drown.

Finally she spoke: "Where are my rings?"

I didn't have a clue what she was talking about. "What rings?"

"You know what rings! My wedding and engagement rings!"

"I don't know." I was completely bewildered.

"You *do* know! Where are they?"

I started to stammer out the truth yet again—*I don't know anything about your rings*—but I was still caught by her black gaze, and I found I didn't dare to speak the truth. Something I saw there in the darkness of her eyes told me I had to protect myself, save myself. If I didn't, she might slap me . . . stop loving me . . . abandon me.

"I took them!" I blurted.

Instantly, something shifted in her expression. Her face grew calm. "Where are they?"

I tried to think. What would make sense? "I took them down to the park," I said, pleased to have come up with such a likely sounding story. "So Sara and I could play house with them."

She nodded, as though this were exactly what she had hoped I would say. Then she grabbed my arm and pulled me down the stairs. Together, we retraced my steps to the park, all the while searching for the rings on the sidewalk, in the street, under cars. I played my role in the charade with desperate eagerness. When we reached the park, I crawled on my hands and knees around the grassy spot where Sara and I had played, looking for the rings I knew were not there.

Crouched there on my hands and knees, I couldn't help but remember how happy I had been in this same spot only a few moments before. Something strange and bad was happening now, something I couldn't explain. My five-year-old mind knew this was a kind of make-believe, but not the happy kind I played with Sara. I glanced up at my mother, quickly, and then I bent my head again. I went back to searching through the grass for the rings. Even though I knew the rings weren't there—how could they be?—a small, crazy piece of my mind was convinced I *would* find the rings, there in the grass where I had somehow left them.

My mother watched me search. After a few moments, when I had found nothing, she turned to go, and I followed her. Without a word between us, we walked back home.

That night when I went to kiss my father before bed, he turned his head away. I flinched as though he'd struck me. I knew he knew about the rings. But *what* did he know? He didn't know the truth: that I was innocent.

I was filled with a confused shame. I was too small to understand, too young to realize my mother must have lost the rings herself. In order to avoid my father's anger, she had made me her scapegoat.

All I knew was that I felt guilty and sad. My father didn't love me the way he once had.

***

We never again spoke of the rings. I never tried to tell my father the truth. Little by little, my voice had less and less to say. I was slowly, even then when I was so young, losing my faith in my own voice. As I did, I lost the sense I'd always had, that a loving Someone kept me company, singing with me.

Meanwhile, other things in my life were changing. When I was seven years old, my brother Nicky was born. Soon after his birth, rheumatoid arthritis struck my mother, and her doctor predicted she would never walk again. Eventually, she would prove him wrong, but in the meantime, I heard my father, grandmother, and aunts talking about her in hushed, shaken voices. Our small apartment was crowded now with medications, heat lamps, and relatives.

No child wants to see her mother lying on the kitchen table under a heat lamp, like a rotisserie chicken at the supermarket! I understand now that the warmth was intended to soothe her crippled muscles and hasten a cure, but as a child, I was terrified.

I prayed each night as the nuns had taught me at school: I asked the Blessed Virgin to make my mother well. And then each morning, I'd watch as my mother tried to get out of bed, gingerly placing one foot and then the other on the floor. Almost instantly, she'd collapse back onto the bed. But she was a stubborn woman. "I've got to walk," she'd mutter between her teeth. "I have two children. One is an infant. I have to walk!"

My father hired a young woman to take care of my brother on the days my grandmother couldn't come to our house. Each day when I came home from school, I would be sent outside immediately to walk alongside the woman while she pushed Nicky in his carriage. My mother undoubtedly craved a few more minutes of quiet to nurse her strength, but I felt as though I were being shuttled aside—and I blamed the woman. I hated her for taking me away from my mother. For me, she became the symbol of all that had gone wrong in my life. I wanted to get rid of her.

One day, I put my hands on my hips and told her we didn't need her anymore. If she didn't leave, I told her, I'd tell my father that she did horrible things. As stricken with guilt as I often was as a child, I don't remember feeling a speck of remorse for my lie. Children can be cruel, and I was no exception. Like many children, I was also powerless—and I was angry! The young woman was my scapegoat, just as I had been my mother's. The woman did leave eventually, not because of my childish threats but because my parents could no longer afford her. Her departure gave me little satisfaction, though.

Somehow, I sensed, my mother blamed me for her pain. Anger, guilt, and fear were my constant companions, like cold, ever-present judges looming over me in their dark robes. Desperate to appease them, I worked hard to save up enough allowance to buy my mother a present for Mother's Day.

By the time May rolled around, I had a sizable sum squirreled away. I pondered what would be the perfect gift. My experience of the world was limited to my family life and the movies I occasionally watched—and one afternoon, sitting in a dark movie theater, I noticed that the beautiful leading lady was wearing something flimsy and pretty as she went to bed. An idea popped into my head: since my mother was in bed most of the time, nightclothes would surely be the perfect gift for her!

I wasn't old enough to travel into Manhattan alone, so I was delighted when I saw exactly what I wanted in a neighborhood shop: a pink satin bed jacket with beige lace sewn into tiny rosebuds around the collar and sleeves. Even the buttons were covered in satin. With a sense of joy and relief—here at last was something I could do for my mother that would surely fill her with happiness and love—I sauntered up to the counter and made my purchase like a veteran shopper.

On Mother's Day morning, I hopped up and down with excitement as I gave my mother her present. She opened it, glanced at the satin confection, and then set it aside.

"What am I going to do with this?" Her expression told me I had done something utterly foolish. "I don't wear these things. Take it back to the store. Get your money back."

Somehow, I had done something terribly wrong. The excitement inside me faded into a dull ache. Then, slowly, even that ache faded away. I became numb.

I was learning not to feel too much.

✳✳✳

Life became more complicated that summer. My mother still couldn't walk, my brother was growing fast, and our one-bedroom apartment was crowded. I slept on a cot in the living room, which only added to the clutter. To help us, my father's sister, Angie, offered to take me home with her for the summer.

At first, I was happy to go. I'd be able to play with my cousins, and I thought it might be fun. But although my aunt was good to me, I soon grew homesick. She listened to me cry myself to sleep every night until she had had enough. Then she took me home.

My father and grandmother were glad to see me, I remember, but it was my mother's reaction that took me by surprise. At the sound of my voice, she came out of her bedroom with her arms outstretched. "My baby, my baby!" Tears streamed down her cheeks.

I too burst into tears, but I didn't dare go to her. I didn't know what to do, I didn't know how to react. This was so out of character for my mother that I was bewildered. And I was terrified I would once again do something wrong.

"Marietta, go and kiss your mother," my aunt said.

Now that I knew what to do, I went to my mother and gave her a kiss.

The memory of that day is still an open question in my mind: Did my mother really love me when I was a child, after all? Or were her tears and outstretched arms all for show, so her sister-in-law, her husband, and her mother would pity her? Like my father who spent his life fondling the memory of his mother's greeting when he came from Italy, I too spent years going over and over in my mind my mother's reaction to my homecoming. I pondered various interpretations. Lacking other evidence of her love, this one moment took on enormous significance.

That night my godmother offered to take me home with her. She lived only four blocks away from my parents, and I agreed to go just for that night. Deep inside, I wanted to get away again from my mother with her confusing emotions. But I felt guilty for feeling that way.

That night, for the first time, I sensed dimly that I was carrying an ever-growing bundle, a tangled mass of guilt, shame, and pain my mother had handed me. *You're a bad little girl.* That was the message she was constantly telling me, both with her words and her actions. *You're spoiled, and you're selfish, and you're naughty.* I never doubted that my mother was right about me, but the knowledge hurt too much to face.

A still deeper numbness crept over me. I stuffed the ugly bundle away where I wouldn't have to look at it. I tried to forget it existed.

But I was lonely. At last, hungry for affection, desperate to escape my sense of guilt, I turned with a new urgency to the faith the nuns taught me at school. There I saw love, security, hope.

Like a diver who throws herself over a cliff into the sea, I plunged into religion.

2

Forget about the thorn in your foot.
Instead, gaze in wonder at the infinite rose garden.
Rumi

I am the rose. . . .
—Song of Solomon 2:1

When I had entered St. Frances of Rome Elementary School in the Bronx, the Sisters had taught me to recite many other prayers besides "Now I Lay Me Down to Sleep." No one explained what the words of the prayers meant, though. Understanding and meaning, the nuns assumed, would come later; for now the words themselves were enough. And so I had learned to say the Our Father, the Hail Mary, and various other prayers all well-educated Catholic school children knew in the 1940s. By this time, I recited them glibly and automatically, believing deeply all the while that they were like powerful magic incantations, words that somehow made God and Mary look on me with favor.

26

Prayers weren't all that the Church offered me during those years of my childhood. There were the Sacraments as well.

Children received their first Holy Communion early in those days. I had barely turned six when, dressed as a mini-bride without a veil (we wore a wreath of leaves instead, symbolizing Jesus' crown of thorns), I opened my mouth like a baby bird and received Jesus' body— in the form of a soft morsel of bread that immediately stuck to the roof of my mouth. I desperately wanted to dislodge it with my tongue, but the nuns had told us that this was absolutely forbidden, tantamount to committing mortal sin. I knew of course that the Sacrament of Penance (which we called Confession in those days) was like a giant sin-eraser, but I didn't want to risk it. I let the bread dissolve in its own good time. I already had the feeling God was not someone with whom you fooled around.

That feeling became even stronger two years later. Then, at the tender age of eight, the Sisters commanded me to stand still while the bishop conferred the sacrament of Confirmation. I couldn't help thinking that the red-robed bishop looked like Santa ready to pounce on a reindeer. Instead, he slapped me across the face. The slap was part of the ceremony, representing my initiation into the Army of Christ. I was supposed to become a soldier now, courageous and strong, in order to preach the Gospel. The Church Triumphant had risen to new heights in the 1940s, and foremost in all Catholic children's training was the discipline of mission and self-sacrifice.

The slap didn't actually hurt much, but the fear and anxiety I'd felt waiting for it magnified the pain a hundredfold in my young mind. My stomach was upset for the rest of the day. Even my consolation prizes—a bouquet of red roses and a party attended by every relative I could claim—didn't calm me. I managed, however to dutifully express my gratitude to everyone who had come to the party. Just as dutifully, I also stated my pride at now being a soldier in the army of Christ.

As I grew older, the Sisters continued to impress on me all I needed to do to become a good Catholic. Attending daily Mass and receiving Holy Communion were essential, not only for myself but for the world. My personal devotion, the nuns informed me, was tied to the entire world's salvation. Unquestioning, I squared my shoulders and accepted the new weight being added to the bundle of guilt and responsibility I was already carrying. I suppose it made sense to me: after all, if my mother's happiness somehow depended on my actions, why not the entire world's as well?

And yet it wasn't always easy for me to do everything the nuns expected—not because I was unwilling, but because I had the double responsibility of pleasing both the Church *and* my parents. My mother and father were not as convinced as I was that the good Sisters always knew best. In order to attend morning Mass, I had to begin my day before dawn, which didn't sit well with my parents. They disapproved of this act of piety that interfered with their sleep, and they scolded me when I insisted I needed to attend Mass daily. I found myself in the awkward position of being caught between my parents' demands and the nuns'.

Ultimately, I found a way to please them both: each morning, I secretly washed, dressed, and tiptoed sock footed to the apartment door. I held my breath, so that the proverbial pin wouldn't drop. When I reached the elevator down the hall, I slipped on my shoes. No one knew I was gone until it was too late.

By the time I was in the eighth grade, my last year at St. Frances of Rome School, my parents had grown accustomed to my early rising. They might not have been pleased, but I no longer faced their active disapproval. Freed from this tension, that spring I noticed for the first time the beauty of those early mornings when I stepped out of our apartment building into the street.

The Bronx, that gritty urban borough, has the perfect soil for roses. On those early treks to Mass, rosebushes blossomed along the fronts of apartment buildings and between attached houses. Climbing roses made intricate patterns along fences. Dew hung like crystal on the briars and the red, yellow, and pink petals. I walked along a tree-lined street, beneath leaves like tiny umbrellas, breathing the scent of roses.

As I walked, I prayed to Mary with all my heart. I didn't pray for my family, or for things, or for better grades. Instead, I asked that if I ever strayed from Mary or her Son, she would bring me home again. Looking back, I realize how unusual this prayer was for a thirteen-year-old.

I was a strange girl, I suppose, anxious and overly sensitive. My superego was already so ponderous it could have sunk the *Titanic* all over again.

Despite all that, the song that so obstinately wove itself throughout my life was the answer to my prayer. Over the years, the song would grow faint; it would lead me to unexpected places; but it never became completely silent. It was the *lit motif* of my life, deeper and more important than any formal prayer I'd been taught to recite. At thirteen, though, I had no words for this knowledge. I had no idea where the future would lead me, and I could not have imagined a way to God other than the one the Sisters taught me.

Equally unaware that my longing for the comfort of a mother's love fueled my devotion, I turned to Mary more and more. On that long-ago day when my mother accused me of taking her rings, I had glimpsed something behind my mother's familiar features, something more terrifying to me than any fairy-tale witch—but the Blessed Virgin's face was always gentle and welcoming, always loving and accepting. I prayed to Mary with an intense, nearly desperate adoration.

Each morning after Mass, I knelt in front of her statue. There, before school began, I said a few prayers, not formal ones but words I had chosen on my own.

Praying to Mary, the Sisters taught, would increase our devotion to God, and she would give us girls a role model for how we too should behave. I gathered that praying to Mary was somehow easier than praying to

God. Mary was a soft touch, a tolerant mother who loved without judgment. Asking her help was far less risky than approaching the powerful and easily angered God the Father. Besides, the nuns said, Jesus would deny his mother nothing. The implication, of course, was that Jesus and the Father would have happily rejected my prayers—but for Mary's sake, they would deign to listen to me.

Mary's image was deeply imprinted on my consciousness. Each May, Mary's month, the students honored her with a procession down the church's center aisle, scattering pink rose petals as we made our way to her statue. While the tiniest girl in the school placed a crown of pink roses on Mary's head, I joined my voice in song with the other girls: "Oh Mary we crown thee with blossoms today! Queen of the Angels, Queen of the May!"

We also reenacted the story of Mary's presentation in the Temple. Oral tradition has it that Ann and Joachim, Mary's parents, brought her to the Temple when she was very young to consecrate her to God. Since our Sisters were members of the Order of the Presentation of the Blessed Virgin Mary, this was an especially important event for them to remember. We girls processed down the church aisle, again strewn with pink rose petals, and when we reached the main altar, a girl playing Mary's role climbed the few steps to the simulated Temple (a spot in front of the altar). The girl knelt, folded her hands, and prayed, while the rest of us responded, "Lord, hear our prayer." As the choirboys' voices filled the church with the soft strains of "Ave Maria," my eyes would fill with tears of love and joy.

Lest after all that we might have still forgotten Mary's preeminence, at our Confirmation each girl took "Mary" as her Confirmation name (unlike the boys who were allowed to choose their own names). I never stopped to consider the irony of being initiated into the Army of Christ at the same moment I also accepted the name of a woman known for her submission and love! Emotionally, I identified far more with Mary than I did with the Church Militant. I accepted gladly, without a question, that Mary had become a part of my very identity.

After our Confirmation, Mary was not forgotten, even during the weeks between her holy days. Every Monday afternoon after school, we students attended Novenas in her honor. We invoked her help in every aspect of life; we especially begged her to grant world peace, a topic much on our minds in those post-World War II years. When the priest took the Eucharist—the thin white wafer we believed was the actual body of Christ—out from the tabernacle, the little gold box where it lived, I sang with the other students, "Immaculate Mary our hearts are on fire." The priest then placed the wafer in a gleaming gold vessel shaped like a sunburst—a monstrance—so he could bless us with it as he carried it around the church. "O Mary," we sang, "our life, our sweetness, and our hope, conceived without sin, pray for us!"

And to top it all off, the final icing on the Mary cake, all of us girls would wear the same blue dresses at our graduation ceremony, clothing ourselves in Mary's favorite color. Like every good Western Catholic, I knew that Mary had worn blue on each of her appearances on Earth. (I didn't know it then, but according to Greek iconography, Mary was also fond of red—and in her appearances at Lourdes and Fatima, she wore white.)

Mary became the foundation of my life. As a Catholic girl growing up in the 1950s, she seemed to surround me with her presence. Through her, I experienced the only freedom and security I knew. Meanwhile, apart from Mary, I faced restrictions everywhere I turned, at home, at school, and at church. These restrictions buttressed my already weighty superego; I judged myself unmercifully for my failure to keep the many rules that had taken up residence in my mind. Mary was my only solace.

And so each morning after Mass, there I'd be on the left side of the altar, kneeling at the communion rail in front of Mary's image. She held her hands open and outstretched, as if she were welcoming me. I would gaze up at her deep blue robe over her white undergarment, at her calm eyes, and most of all at her gentle lips, and I would yearn to speak to her as I would to a friend.

One morning when I came to Mary, I found that the sacristan—the man whose job was to tend to the altar—had placed vases of lilacs on each side of her statue. Their delicate scent filled my senses as I looked up at her face, just as I always did. But this time something was different.

Mary smiled at me.

I looked again—and then again. I was a fairly bright kid, and I knew that make-believe and reality were two different things. I assumed this experience must fall into the first category. And yet I was convinced Mary's smile widened as I watched, a soft, loving smile that must surely be meant only for me.

It had to be my imagination. What else could it be? Still, I yearned to remain there, gazing at Mary's face. I had to get to class, but happiness was like a steady melody humming inside me the rest of the day.

The next morning, I went eagerly to the altar and knelt. I looked up at Mary—and she smiled again. I didn't know what to make of it; I only knew I was supremely happy. I wanted to kneel there in front of her forever. I had never before felt such love and compassion directed toward me. This time, I didn't care if I'd be late for school. I couldn't bear to leave this haven of security and joy.

Eventually, I had to go, of course. As I once more immersed myself in the day's routine, I again attributed the experience to my imagination. I dared not think it might be real.

The next morning, as I knelt gazing up at Mary's smiling face, I knew with every fiber of my being that this *was* real. Her smile told me something I had never believed: I was good.

And I was loved.

I was afraid to tell anyone. I knew they'd think I was crazy. Or they might think I was arrogant or a liar, someone who simply craved attention. Yet I felt I had been given a gift, a gift to be held and guarded, hidden from everyone. I didn't want to lose it.

And then one morning, I did lose it. I approached the altar as eagerly as ever and looked up into Mary's face—but her smile was gone. I strained my eyes, pressed my body against the rail until it hurt, hoping I could force a smile from her.

Nothing happened.

I went to her the next day, and the day after that, and for weeks afterward, hoping against hope her smile would return. It never did. Instead, her mouth seemed to have twisted into a scowl. Her entire face showed displeasure now. I was sure I had done something terribly wrong. Why else wouldn't she smile at me?

In the months that followed, I came to believe I'd never see her smile again. The pain cut through the numbness I had cultivated. I wasn't sure I could bear it.

As I grew older, however, I learned again to hide my pain from myself. I was a well-educated young woman, and I became quite clinical about the experience. I knew I had never believed my biological mother loved me, knew that I had always wistfully watched and envied my friends' loving mothers. No wonder I had projected a smile onto a statue's face! I was simply creating the ideal mother I had always wanted, finding a way to give my yearning self the love it craved. The loss of that smile meant nothing except that I was growing up.

✳✳✳

A life is not a novel. When we look back, we usually can't see that one moment leads to the next in a logical pattern that builds to a climax and then a dénouement. Instead, although we live our lives in a linear fashion, our memories become jumbled. Their chronological connections are edited from our minds. We remember isolated moments, and we lay them out in first one pattern and then another. But we have no way of knowing which is "real." In a sense, they all are—and none of them are.

I don't know how Mary's smile connected to the other events going on in my life. I can only choose to believe her smile was a visible version of the song I had always heard. One way or another, the loss of her smile was connected to the widening gap between my inner voice and my sense of my outer identity.

I was still singing, though, with a voice that now had the dramatic range of a spinto soprano. (In an opera, a spinto soprano can sing both lyric and dramatic parts.) My parents were proud of my voice, which made me happy. And I was ecstatic when they decided I needed music lessons. I opted to attend those lessons rather than see my friends, go to the movies, or do just about anything.

My teacher was a man in his late sixties who had been coaching singers and pianists for years. My parents liked him: he was Italian. He even taught nuns, so naturally, they reasoned, he must be a good man. At first, he gave me piano instruction, because my voice was not yet mature enough for singing lessons, but when I turned thirteen, the same year I found and lost Mary's smile, I gave up the piano instruction and began voice lessons instead. My parents couldn't afford both.

In the beginning, I sang nothing but scales and exercises. As time went by and my voice gained power and flexibility, my teacher allowed me to choose a song to sing from an operetta or musical comedy. Since I was doing so well, he then introduced me to opera. That was when things changed.

3

One day, you will no longer live in shame.
Don't be intimidated; all your humiliation will disappear.
You will no longer remember the shame of your youth.
Isaiah 54:4

One day my music teacher told me if I wanted to learn to sing with the same fire the great sopranos had, I'd have to learn a technique that many opera stars used. Before each performance, he said, the leading man—or for that matter, any man—would place his hands on strategic parts of the singer's body. This, he said, would improve the quality and range of her voice. Her voice would ring out like a bell.

I had just reached adolescence. I was interested in boys, but I was innocent enough not to know where babies came from. In today's world, this seems incredible, but I honestly still thought angels delivered babies while parents slept. I was attending a Catholic school, steeped in religion and study, protected from "worldly" distractions, and I was also a daughter in a protective

Italian household. So as I listened to my teacher, it never occurred to me that he was lying. After all, he gave piano lessons to nuns!

Shyly, I agreed to undergo the "technique" he urged me to try. At the next lesson, the lesson after that, and for weeks to come, I stood awkwardly while the man fondled me. At first, I felt only embarrassment. Eventually, I grew to hate the experience. I also hated him. But I told no one what was happening, except my best friend, Doris. I begged her not to tell anyone, and she agreed. I knew now that what my teacher was doing was "something bad"—but I felt I was to blame. Shame filled me with a near-constant nausea.

Then one afternoon, my mother confronted me out of the blue. "Is what Doris told me true? Is it?"

I could only stare at her, horrified, frozen yet again by those black eyes of hers.

"Is it?" she demanded. "Because if it is, your father will get a gun and shoot him! Remember, you have to walk down the aisle with a veil over your face!" Wearing a veil over your face on your wedding day meant you were a virgin. Anyone who wasn't a virgin was soiled, sinful, a shame to her family.

I pasted on a shaky smile and said, "Oh Mom, you know Doris, she's always so dramatic. She just exaggerated something I told her. It wasn't anything like that." I gulped, searching for something that would both appease her and distract her. "But anyway," I forced myself to say in a gay, airy voice, "I don't want to take lessons from him anymore. I want to take lessons from a *real* opera star. Then I can *really* learn to sing."

Her expression lightened instantly, and I sucked in a long breath of relief. My shame, however, was still there, a dark film that clung to me so stubbornly I knew I would never be able to peel it off, even if no one ever knew, even if I never had to see my music teacher again.

✳✳✳

My relationship with my mother had always been difficult, tenuous and precarious even at its best, but until now, I had usually felt more relaxed with my father. My love for him was a far simpler thing than what I felt for my mother. He was the parent who read me stories at bedtime when I was small. He took me to baseball games, and we went fishing together. On Sunday mornings after church, we'd visit the Botanical Gardens in the Bronx, where he taught me the names of flowers and trees. Afterward, he'd buy us ice cream cones, and we would sit on a bench, licking our favorite flavors while he talked about the beauty of nature.

He was always interested in my schoolwork, and he took time to look at my homework every day. He even dickered with the nuns over a point or two on my final grades (although I consistently made the honor roll anyway). I thought he was the most intelligent man in the world, and when I was small, I felt safe with him. So long as I held his hand, I believed, nothing would harm me.

My sense of security had been shaken after the incident with my mother's rings. Then, when I reached adolescence—somewhere around the same time that my voice teacher was introducing me to his technique, as well as the same time I was becoming convinced I had lost Mary's love forever—something shifted in my relationship with my father. He still gave me a hug and a kiss when he came home from work, but I sensed he had pulled away from me. Psychologists have written a good deal about fathers and their adolescent daughters, but what happened with my father still seems to me to have been something different from the normal changes that come to any father-daughter relationship. He himself altered in some dark way. He was suddenly unpredictable and irritable, and his cruelty was directed at my brother as often as at me.

I still took for granted, though, that I was "Daddy's girl"—until one night as I was about to fall asleep, I heard my parents quarreling. My mother's voice said, "Don't think your daughter is so good. She. . ." I missed the rest of her words, but almost immediately, I heard my father stomp down the hallway toward my room.

I pulled the blankets over my head as he flung open the door, but he yanked back the covers. "No, Daddy, no!" I screamed as he struck me on the head, back and forth with his hands. Then, just as suddenly, he was gone again.

I never knew what I had done wrong. I didn't ask. My sense of shame and fear grew heavier, and without protest, I accepted the additional weight on my shoulders.

All Italian parents are protective of their daughters, but my father's attitude toward me grew increasingly irrational. One night, I got a ride home with some friends after a play rehearsal at church; as always, whenever I was out, my parents were watching for my return from our apartment window. One of the young men in the car, a friend of mine from church, got out with me to say good-bye. He was a sailor who was leaving for overseas duty the next day, so I gave him a quick kiss on his cheek.

When I came upstairs and opened the door to my apartment, I found my parents waiting for me. Without a word, my father leapt forward and slapped me across the face. The blow was hard enough to knock me on the floor.

"You tramp!" he shouted. "What will the neighbors think—getting out of a car with a *sailor*. *Kissing* a sailor. Why you—" He gave me a kick as I lay crying on the floor. "All those years in a Catholic school, and you act like this? Go to bed—before I really give you something to cry about!"

From that day on, I lived in fear of my father. He still acted loving to me sometimes, but my fear of him never left me. From then on, for more than fifty years, until my father died at the age of ninety-eight, I was never free of that fear.

I became convinced I carried something shameful inside me, something that turned people against me. My mother had betrayed me long ago when she accused me of stealing her ring. My voice teacher had betrayed me by abusing me sexually; my best friend Doris had betrayed me by telling my mother my secret; and now my father, the person I had thought would always keep me safe, had betrayed me as well.

At the same time, I felt I deserved their betrayal.

I had a new music teacher now, so I no longer had to submit to the weekly molestation, but the stain on my sense of self remained. For the first time, singing and shame were linked in my mind. I was still too young to make sense of the events in my life—the changes in my father, the sexual abuse, my experience with Mary—and too confused to draw the logical conclusions that would probably have been obvious to an outsider. I was certain I was the one at fault. Why else would even Mary the Mother of God have betrayed me too?

I didn't want to feel betrayed by Mary. Without her, there was nowhere else to turn. I could no longer say the rosary, or look at her statues and paintings, let alone pray to her the way I once had. The scent of roses no longer filled me with joy. Instead, I was filled with shame and a terrible anxiety that never left me.

In the end, Mary was just one more person who had rejected me.

***

My new voice teacher had sung at La Scala in Italy, and she was the stereotypical opera star: a big-bosomed lady draped in brilliant colors, black hair adorned with jeweled clips, with a speaking voice that was nearly indistinguishable from her singing voice. I adored her. She was patient and kind, and she brought out parts of my voice I hadn't known existed, parts that came from deep within me. What she taught me felt magical. Singing was still my only hope, the only way I could connect to that sense of Someone who loved me, no matter what. And so I did my best to bury the shame I felt whenever I felt my chest swell with song.

I was diligent about my voice lessons, I still found joy in them . . . but nevertheless, singing was growing more and more difficult for me. In fact, practicing at home had become sheer torture. Adolescent boys and opera aren't exactly compatible, and my brother and his friends loved to tease me. Whenever they saw me in the street, they would burst into dramatic trills, imitating my voice. Meanwhile, my father hovered over me while I practiced, analyzing every note I sang. Although he knew little about music himself, he was quick to point out when he believed I was off key or if I sang too loud or too soft. "You're in bad voice today," he'd tell me.

Singing was no longer the simple joy it had once been. Despite my teacher's encouragement, eventually I could barely hear the Someone who sang with me anymore. The critical voices around me were just too loud.

✳✳✳

I was trying to be the best Catholic schoolgirl I could—but I was also an adolescent. As boys, dances, and parties became increasingly important to me, my "impure" thoughts filled me with guilt. "Holding a kiss longer than two seconds is a mortal sin," the Sisters claimed, but I had discovered that kisses longer than two seconds were actually quite pleasurable. I desperately wanted to live inside the thick boundary lines the nuns had drawn for me, and yet at the same time, a secret, defiant rebellion was growing within me. It did nothing to diminish my guilt. Quite the contrary. I walked through life feeling I needed to be cleansed for simply being alive. I broke one small rule after another—and I agonized over each one.

My guilt was compounded during the winter months. The drab days made my inner darkness harder to bear. Worries about the future tormented me: What would I do when I grew up? Would I be able to get a job? Who would hire me? How would I survive? I loved the theatre, and I longed for a career on stage—but everyone knew theatre people starved most of the time. Besides, when I had mentioned my aspirations to my mother, her response had been, "No daughter of mine is going to become a tramp, acting on the stage."

During warmer weather, I could distract myself from my worries—but life was joyless and gray during those winter months. To ease the pain, I played hooky from school and then wandered through the streets, schoolbag in hand, digging my boots into the dirty snow hour after hour until the movie houses opened. I didn't care what movie was playing, so long as it helped me forget my own life for a while. As the fantasy world unfurled on the screen, I sat in the darkness eating candy . . . and then more candy. I watched the same movie over and over again, and then managed to arrive home precisely at the same time in the afternoon as if I had attended school. The next day I would bring a note to school that said I'd been sick the day before, forged in my mother's handwriting.

No one ever caught me, but my guilt grew heavier. I couldn't admit my crimes to anyone, and at the same time, I couldn't stop seeking the only escape I knew how to find. My guilt swelled to enormous proportions. I longed for some release from my shame—and so, like a drunk groping in the dark for a drink, I turned to the confessional.

I found churches in Manhattan where confessions were heard between six and eight in the mornings, before the beginning of school, and now I woke up and left our apartment even earlier. I explained my early-morning departures to my parents by claiming I needed to do research in the school library. Going to confession became an almost daily routine. It was one more secret I kept, as much of an addiction as playing hooky.

After confession, I would ride to school on the Third Avenue El. The elevated tracks ran close to apartment tenements, so close I could see through the windows to the rooms inside. The same scenes rushed past me every morning, glimpses of entire families sleeping in one room, hallways strewn with dirty laundry and empty bottles of alcohol, gray faces turned toward the windows as the El roared by them.

My background and education separated me from these people. They seemed to me like animals trapped inside cages—and yet I found myself identifying with them. At some level, I believed they *were* me. Surely, it was only a matter of time until my outer life was the same as my inner life—and then my life would look like theirs. I would never be employed because no one would hire me. Who would want to when at my most secret core I was so evil? Once I entered the grown-up world, I was convinced, all my secrets would be revealed—and I would end up living in tenements like these or in the streets, a prostitute, an alcoholic, or something worse.

Morning after morning, I shivered on the train, thinking these thoughts until, despite the cold, I'd start to sweat. My heart pounded. I knew I had only myself to blame for the horrible person I had become. I hadn't measured up; I would be punished.

I imagined my mother, my father, and God, high in the sky, a stern Trinity condemning me as they looked down, waiting for what I'd do next. At other times, they seemed like the puppet masters that held the strings of my life. I couldn't move unless they pulled the strings. I was helpless, powerless. I was nothing.

And yet I survived. No one guessed how unhealthy my inner thoughts had become. Outwardly, I was lots of fun, always kidding around, playing jokes on my friends, making fun of authority figures. Sometimes my friends teased me when they found me with my nose in some thick, dull book of philosophy, psychology, or theology, but I laughed them off. Secretly, I was seeking the answer to the question I most feared: "How will it all end?" When my shame was revealed, what then?

Despite this constant guilty terror, I did well in school. I earned good grades, and better yet, I was the lead in my high school's operettas four years in a row. Acting and singing on stage were the only times I was truly happy, and the response I received from the audience over-whelmed me. They loved me and I knew it. I, in turn, loved them, so grateful was I for their love.

I could not believe in my own talent, though. I wrote a letter to my drama coach: "Do I have enough talent for a career on the stage? Am I only fooling myself? Please, be brutally honest with me." Her affirmation in response to my letter made me ecstatic, but my fears remained.

I daydreamed about going to a drama school after graduation from high school. I imagined myself living in Greenwich Village, finding a job that would pay the rent while I went to auditions.

But who was I kidding? One word to my parents about plans like these, and I could kiss good-bye any notion that they would fund my education, let alone allow me to still consider myself a part of their family. "If you want a career as a singer," my mother told me, "it has to be opera—or nothing. Opera is the only respectable way for a young woman to perform."

But opera wasn't what I wanted; I loved musical com-edies. So I didn't give up, not yet.

4

Do you know what the music is saying?
"Don't worry, you will find the way.
Even your mistakes are leading you to the Truth."
Rumi

I got a job as a tour guide at Rockefeller Center, working after school, on weekends, and during the summers, saving my money. My hours were flexible enough that I could go to auditions during the day and on weekends.

At the end of every audition, the verdict was always the same: "You have a leading lady's voice, but you're too short. Besides you have dark hair, and your skin isn't fair enough. You'd be better suited for character parts—but you'll have to change your voice to sound more like Mary Martin or Ethel Merman."

Back then, stereotypes shaped a singer's choices. I didn't care. Something inside me was still stubborn enough to keep trying. My voice wanted to be heard.

On my own, using my own money, I found myself a vocal coach, a man who happened to also be coaching Barbra Streisand and Julie Andrews. Working with him felt like a miracle, each moment precious and amazing. He taught me techniques I had never learned from my opera singer, how to "put over a song." Music and lyrics were so intertwined that each supported the other, and I could sing and act simultaneously. The experience was a heady, tantalizing taste of the power I longed for.

I also made up my mind to take ballet lessons to firm my muscles and make me more comfortable with the dance moves I needed for acting in musicals. Again, I paid for the lessons myself. My family never knew; I was still keeping my secrets. This time, though, I was rebelling all over the place—and having a grand time in the process. Despite the guilt and shame that never went away, that beloved Someone was reaching out to me again, singing to me through my own voice.

I graduated from high school and, still living at home, went to Fordham University. At first, I had been happy to attend Fordham because of its theatre department— but as luck would have it, the university decided to drop its drama program my freshman year. Too many professional theater people—avant-garde types dressed in black, waving long cigarette holders—were hovering around Fordham's Catholic halls. The university didn't want to risk the worldly contamination.

Instead, I settled for a communication arts major, which consisted of courses in radio, television, journalism, and some theatre. I was the first woman at the university to take this major, and since young women were not normally allowed to attend courses on the main campus (they went instead to the School of Education in downtown Manhattan), I had to get special permission from both the university's president and the diocesan bishop. Only then was I allowed to be the one young woman in classrooms full of young men.

The major turned out to not be so bad. In my freshman year, I played in *You Can't Take It with You*, and each year after that, I acted in one of Chekhov's one-act plays. I performed in a series of radio plays as well, and when I was a junior, I had my own radio show, *Marietta's Guest Room*. My job for the show was to interview people— teachers, administrators, some media people—anyone who might be important to the university in one way or another. I tried to use my sense of humor to make the show as entertaining as possible, but with teachers and administrators, it was like trying to walk an elephant with sewing thread as a leash: the conversations moved in whatever direction the person wanted, despite my best efforts to guide it elsewhere. As a result, the interviews were slow, ponderous . . . and dull.

That same year, though, another opportunity came my way. A Catholic organization was looking for someone to costar in a television show called *The Fourth R*, to be aired on NBC every Sunday morning. (The "fourth R" was religion.) I auditioned and got the part. Television was still new then: everything was done live, and in black and white. Chalk lines on the floor told us where to walk in order to stay in front of the cameras. My costar, a Dominican sister, taught catechism to a live audience of children, and then I led them in a song, told them a story, or read a poem. Sister, the children, and I clicked in some magical way, and the show was a success.

Through all these experiences, no one guessed the guilt I harbored inside or the sense of hypocrisy I felt whenever I performed on *The Fourth R*. Who was I to teach impressionable young minds about God? Who was I to speak to them of God's love when the only God I knew was cold and distant? Who was I to model for them a "good" Christian?

By then, guilt controlled my interior life. I took for granted its tight grip on my thoughts. Today, I can point to my parents, the Church, the society of the day, even my own temperament as contributing to my neurotic guilt, but I'm not sure any of those factors truly explains how unhealthy I had become. Other individuals have experienced the same or very similar conditions as I did. Even the sexual molestation was hardly unique. But for whatever reason, guilt overwhelmed me. I was possessed.

I'm not saying a demonic presence controlled me. It wasn't the kind of possession that requires exorcism. And yet I was me and not-me simultaneously; my head, heart, and body were disconnected from each other. Instead of a healthy alignment between them, each one had its own existence. Outwardly, I seemed to be doing fine. Emotionally, I functioned like a robot much of the time. I had taught myself to be numb, and now I could no longer connect my emotions to my exterior life. All I could feel was guilt, and so I lived inside my head. I enjoyed intellectual exercises, but my feelings were frozen—and those I could still feel felt distant, as though they were voices calling to me from far away. In a strange way, I no longer perceived any "I" in me. Since I lacked that interior volition, I had no way to choose something different. My inner voice was nearly gone.

And yet, for a while at least, I continued to sing and take voice lessons. Singing still gave me my only hope of safety in a chaotic world. On the El, standing in the swaying space between the cars, I would let my voice pour out where no one could hear it. The vibration of my own voice within my throat gave me hope.

And then, sometime in my senior year at college, I began to lose my singing voice. Thinking I had chronic laryngitis, I went to doctors and then throat specialists. They all concluded there was nothing physically wrong with me.

Now, my voice teacher spent at least half of each lesson helping me regain my voice. By the time I finally did, I had only a few minutes left to sing. I left each lesson filled with hope that my voice was back for good, but inevitably, after a few days, it would disappear again. By the time I went back for another lesson, I would have to go through it all again. Week after week was the same.

Finally, it was too frustrating and painful to keep trying. I gave up. My dream of a career in the theatre had been a childish one, I told myself, totally impractical. The faint stubborn voice inside me finally grew quiet. I let myself become entirely numb. I didn't want to care anymore.

By this time, I was also engaged to be married. I told my parents that continuing to spend money on singing lessons was ridiculous, when in a couple of months I'd be married. My husband would be attending law school, and I needed to get a job to help support us. Giving up music felt like a relief.

But the loss of my voice haunted me. Deep inside, I believed its loss was connected to my guilt. It was my punishment.

Meanwhile, I didn't know why I was the way I was. I had lost my own story. There were no connections left in my memory that could possibly make sense of my life.

Years later, a therapist told me my father's constant criticism had robbed me of my voice. I'm sure that played a part, but the problem seemed deeper, beyond my ability to describe. I did not understand that I had lost more than my singing voice. The strength and authority I had gained from my own unique creativity was gone. I had lost my connection to the beloved Someone.

What remained was a vague hope that someday, somehow, my voice would miraculously return. I gave up looking for it in the here and now, though. Instead, I settled for the life all good Catholic girls wanted: marriage, a home of my own, and a family.

5

When you see an angry face, look past it.
Remember that each person
reacts differently on life's battlegrounds.
One person may turn and run.
Another, just as scared, fights even more fiercely.
Rumi

I hadn't dated very much during my teenage years, partly because all my attention was focused on my voice, partly because my parents were strict, and partly because I didn't consider myself to be attractive. I was only slightly overweight, but in my own eyes, I could have been a stand-in for Sidney Greenstreet, movies' ultimate fat man in the 1930s and '40s. If a boy paid any attention to me, I'd do a comedy routine to make him laugh; I was convinced my personality and looks alone would never be enough to hold his attention. Instead, he'd like me for the laughs, and I wouldn't have to feel the pain of rejection.

All that had changed during my freshman year of college when I acted alongside a green-eyed young man who had the lead role in *You Can't Take It with You*. He reminded me of the young Orson Welles. (I learned later that Orson himself had told him once, "My God, you look enough like me to be my son.") One night after a rehearsal, the young man asked me for my telephone number. My hand shaking, I wrote my number on the inside of a matchbox. He said he'd call the following Saturday night.

And he did. His name was Henri Pierre, but everyone called him Pete. On our first date, I learned his father was the production stage manager for the musical hit *Guys and Dolls*; his dad's career was what had brought the family to New York from California. His mother had been a café singer in San Francisco, and his brother-in-law was an actor both on the stage and in the movies. His theatrical family intrigued me, of course. Pete, too, wanted to become an actor, although he was also considering becoming a drama critic. Falling in love with him seemed like a doorway to my dreams.

A few months after we started dating, Pete was drafted into the Army to serve in the Korean War. He was stationed in Alaska, but he came home a year later on furlough. We picked up where we had left off and became engaged.

Now that Pete was about to become a family man, however, his father persuaded him against a theatrical career. "The theatre's not a stable life," his father told him. "You'll never have a steady income, and you can't raise a family like that. I don't care how good you are! It's a tougher business than you can imagine."

Pete tried to reason with him. "But Dad, *you've* done okay."

"I've done okay because I was involved in the technical end of the business," was his father's response. "But you want to be an actor. That's a whole different story. Believe me, I know what I'm talking about."

To my enormous disappointment, Pete gave in. He relinquished his acting dreams and applied to Georgetown Law School in Washington, D.C. Once he was out of the Army, he would become a lawyer.

Meanwhile, I had completely given up my own stage career, hoping that somehow, through Pete, I might one day have another chance at acting. When Pete let go of his dreams, my own disappeared as well.

My parents, however, were delighted. They would have a lawyer for a son-in-law, their daughter would give up her silly notions about the theatre, and all would be marvelous.

As the months and weeks passed, however, my uneasiness increased. At first, when Pete returned to Alaska, I wrote to him every day. Weeks passed, then months, without a response. I begged Pete to write to me and explain what had happened between us—but I never got an answer. Finally, engagement or not, I decided to date other men.

When my father found out, he was furious with me. He sat me down on a chair in the dinette, and like a well-seasoned barrister sure of his strategy, he confronted me. "What do you think you're doing? You're engaged to be married! This man will provide for you in every way. If you keep on like this you'll ruin everything! You hear? Everything will be ruined! As long as you're living in my house, you're not to date anyone else! Do you understand me?"

I tried to argue, to explain the situation, to describe my own feelings. But my voice held no power. He didn't even hear me.

Pete came home again eventually, and our engagement continued as though the long space with no communication had never happened. I never knew what it had meant. I worried what it boded for the future. Nevertheless, three months after my graduation from college, we were married.

I had hoped that now at last my parents would be pleased with me. After all, I had taken the path they had chosen for me. But once the happy day had come and gone, my father still wasn't satisfied. Even on my honeymoon to Cape Cod, he called me on the telephone to scold me. "Why do you have to live so far away from us when you come back from your honeymoon? Your mother has been crying ever since the wedding day. She looks in your empty closet and weeps. How could you hurt her like this? Your husband could have chosen a law school nearer to home. Why did you do this to us?"

Any happiness I might have felt was immediately squashed. I had thought by taking the good-girl route and becoming a wife, I would finally escape the guilty burden I carried—but now I discovered it would only grow heavier. No matter how I tried, I could never please my parents.

When we arrived in Washington, I began looking for a job. Pete was attending law school full time, so I needed to work. Unfortunately, only government jobs were to be found in D.C. Despite my degree, I wasn't qualified, since I couldn't type or take shorthand.

A month later, I discovered I wouldn't have to work after all: I was pregnant. Pete switched to evening classes and got a daytime job. It didn't seem like such a big deal to us—many other young couples attending law and medical schools were in the same boat—and I was happy, although a bit anxious. The thought of becoming a mother was overwhelming, but I hoped my parents would be pleased to find out they would be grandparents.

They weren't.

"Why couldn't you have waited?" my mother asked.

"Pete will never be able to finish his law degree now." My father's voice was heavy with disapproval.

"Well, I've had so many disappointments in my life." My mother sighed. "This is just one more."

My father added, "I thought my son-in-law was more of a man!"

Their reaction filled me with new shame, as well as anger. Once again, without even meaning to, I had failed them.

Things changed, though, when their granddaughter was born. They doted on the baby, and for the first time in my life, I felt my mother melting just a little toward me. Maybe I had finally done something that pleased her. Maybe her attention had shifted from me to my daughter Renee. I'm not sure. I do know our relationship changed, ever so slightly.

By the time Pete graduated from law school, I was pregnant again. This time, my parents' reaction was different. Pete was graduating seventh in his class, and all he had to do now was take the bar exam and find a good law firm where he could work. In my parents' mind, this was the "right time" for us to be having a family.

Pete passed the bar and got a position with a Manhattan law firm. We moved back to New York City, my daughter Denise was born, and for the next few years, the four of us lived in an apartment in the Bronx. When we had enough money for a down payment, we bought a home on Long Island. Before long, our third daughter, Nicole, was born.

I loved being with my daughters, but I also had twinges of uneasiness and claustrophobia, especially during the winters when the girls and I were trapped indoors. When my youngest was old enough to go to nursery school, I decided to go back to school for a master's degree in English education. I had no great desire to become a teacher, but it would get me out of the house—and I knew teaching was the perfect profession for a mother: short workdays, the same vacations as my children, and enough paid sick days that I could stay home with the children when they were ill.

Soon after my graduation, I got a job teaching English in a high school close to our home and to the children's schools. Pete, meanwhile, continued to commute to work three hours each day, taking the Long Island Railroad to Manhattan, and then from there a subway to his office. His work hours were long, and he was rarely home to eat dinner with us except on weekends. The pay was good, and he had the opportunity for advancement to a partnership. What else could anyone ask of a father and husband?

I told myself we were happy. I loved my children. My husband had a good job. We had a nice home.

I had nearly forgotten that I had ever had a voice of my own—until, imperceptibly at first, things began to change.

✻✻✻

Pete often came home tired, frustrated, and angry. Meanwhile, the responsibility for running the family fell on me: shopping, meals, driving the children, attending their events, and picking Pete up from the train station morning and night at the most ungodly hours. It was a common story, of course, one that many couples were living during that era.

Like all married couples, we'd always had our arguments. But something different was evolving now, something neither of us had expected nor imagined. Neither of us had a clue why it was happening.

Our arguments had turned violent. At first I wasn't worried about the change in our married life. So what if I screamed and Pete threw things around sometimes? Didn't all families have these moments? My father had been known to overturn the dining room table when he was angry. I had never expected family life to be as calm and sunny as television shows like *Father Knows Best* or *Leave It to Beaver.*

But as the years went by, the violence escalated. Friday evenings were the worst. At the end of the workweek, lawyers often got together for a few drinks to drown the week's tensions. I'd end up picking up Pete from the train station at twelve or one in the morning. He'd be drunk to one degree or another, but it was never a jolly sort of inebriation. Instead, he'd be angry. When we got home, he'd go to bed without a word. I had enough sense not to say anything.

The next morning would be when things got really bad. I could usually sense what was coming from the thud of Pete's footsteps on the stairs as he came down for breakfast. I would brace myself, just as I once had when I heard my father's steps in the hall outside my room. Pete would push me aside as he came into the kitchen and fling open the refrigerator door. Then he'd scramble up some eggs in a bowl and slam the cast-iron frying pan onto the stove.

"Please don't do that," I asked him once.

His only response was to hurl the frying pan straight at me. I ducked in time. After that, I tried to keep my mouth shut.

Sometimes, though, I forgot. When I did, Pete's reaction was swift and unpredictable. Once, he flung his heavy attaché case at me. That time, I didn't move out of the way fast enough. I limped for a week, and I had to make up an excuse about falling on the ice to tell the other teachers at work.

About this time, I found out I was pregnant yet again. This time, the doctor was worried about the pregnancy, and he ordered me to go to bed. As I lay there one day, feeling scared, my mother telephoned. Hearing her voice, I longed for a world where she could make everything right, a world where I could be safe and happy as I had never been in reality. I began to cry.

For whatever reason, my tears set off something in Pete. He snatched the phone from my hand and slammed it down. Then he turned to me. I cowered against my pillow, waiting for whatever came next.

***

I lost the baby that afternoon. After that, something changed inside me. I no longer cringed meekly and silently while Pete raged. Instead, his anger now triggered mine, as though I had succumbed to a deadly contagion he carried, unbottling the years of fury I had stored inside my heart. I felt a perverse pleasure each time I yielded to my rage.

Once my anger had faded, when I couldn't remember what I had said or done, I would be swamped by my old guilt, which would fade away into sadness. My own fury terrified me. I didn't realize that the voice I had smothered for years was screaming for recognition, raging to be heard.

Meanwhile, my husband's frustration was growing too. His workload was enormous, he struggled with his clients, and he never felt his position was secure. Again and again, he failed to make partner at his law firm. He let off steam in explosions that were swift and silent, less verbal than mine and far more physical. I was more afraid of my husband now than I had ever feared my parents. The situation became desperate enough that I called the police.

"Sorry, lady, this is between you and your husband," the officer told me. "We don't get involved in family matters. You gotta work things out for yourself."

I was trapped. Nowhere to go, no safe place to hide, ashamed to tell anyone. I blamed myself for what was happening.

Meanwhile, my children watched their mother scream while their father became increasingly violent. I didn't truly understand the trauma we were inflicting on them. With the resiliency of childhood—and their own innate grace and strength—our daughters survived.

But for Pete and me it was too late. After twenty-one years, our marriage ended.

On the final morning, I drove him to the station for the last time. He lifted his suitcase from the car and gave me a small wave of his hand. "Good-bye." His voice held a grave formality that brought tears to my eyes.

I waited in the car as he walked along the train platform, briefcase in one hand, attaché case in the other. He stopped to buy the New York Times, then leaned against a pole while he waited for the train. I watched till he stepped into the train, and the doors closed behind him. The whistle blew, and the train pulled away.

Even now, I wonder: what happened to our marriage? How could what once held promise and hope end this way? Now, years later, Pete is no longer alive, but I still remember him as a young man full of dreams and passion. Would his life had been different if his father had not pressured him into leaving the theater? Might our marriage have survived if Pete had not experienced such intense stress in a career for which he was not suited? Did he ever, I wonder now, find *his* voice?

But on that day as I sat in the car, realizing that Pete and his anger were no longer a part of my life, I felt as though I were slowly waking up after a long, dark night. I gradually became aware that the sun was shining. The first cool breeze of autumn blew through the open window, and I watched women and children walking to school. A nearby storekeeper sang as he counted the merchandise on display outside his shop. A couple of pumpkins fell off the back of a farm truck. I smiled and started the car.

I drove home, went inside, closed the front door, and looked around. Nothing seemed familiar. It was a stranger's house. I did not recognize my own life.

In the silence, I heard in my mind the lines from Macbeth: "Life is a waking shadow, a poor player who struts and frets his hour upon the stage only to be heard no more. It is a tale told by an idiot, full of sound and fury, signifying nothing."

Surely, I thought, it must mean *something*.

But what?

6

What is this . . .
budding in our hearts?
It is the glorious sound
of a soul waking up.
Hafiz

And where was God in all this? I didn't have a clue.

Through the early years of my marriage, I had continued to be a good Catholic girl. My children received the
sacraments and attended religious instruction; we com-
plied with the Church's teaching on birth control, con-
tributed to charity, and volunteered for church activities.

Now, I wanted to break free of every rule, doctrine,
or dogma that had been thrown at me since I was very
young. I had tried my entire life to be a good girl—and
look what it had got me! The Church had failed me when
I was a child, and now it had failed me as a woman. Both
my marriage and my religion were dead to me. And since
God and the Church were indistinguishable in mind, when
I left the Church, I thought I left God.

That morning after I had said good-bye to Pete, alone in my quiet house, I resolved I would no longer choke back my voice. I made up my mind to become a different person. I didn't know how to go about doing that, but I knew that before I could transform myself into something new, I needed to wake up all the way. When you're asleep, you often don't know you're asleep, you don't know that you're dreaming—and it came to me now that I had to become aware of all the ways I'd been asleep for most of my life.

The process of becoming emotionally and intellectually conscious isn't easy. It's a little like when a limb that's been asleep regains feeling: it feels worse before it feels better. The transformation requires merciless honesty. Meanwhile, the road ahead is elusive. We stumble and fall. We think we have everything all figured out—and then we fall again.

I didn't realize that emotional and intellectual awareness would bring spiritual awakening as well, that the processes were inextricably linked. As the weeks and months went by, however, I was increasingly caught up in a relentless process of spiritual transformation. The process made demands that were far from comfortable. It forced me to look at my own choices, at the life I had created for myself. It refused to be silent.

Gradually, in the months that followed, I became aware of something new (or perhaps it had been there all along?), a silent something that was nevertheless a voice within me. Or maybe it was more like a nudge. I found myself recalling the words of an old poem, "The Hound of Heaven" by Francis Thompson:

I fled Him down the nights and down the days;
I fled Him down the arches of the years;
I fled Him down the labyrinthine ways
Of my own mind; and in the midst of tears
I hid from Him.

I had been running a long time, I realized—and now I was exhausted.

And yet I was still running. Now, though, I sensed, I was running *toward* something. I couldn't map out the path ahead, but I felt that someone was there in the darkness with me, seeking me, calling to me with my own forgotten voice.

***

A year after Pete left, I became involved in the longest school strike in New York State history. We made national headlines.

The strike also made me dead broke. According to New York State law at the time, teachers were penalized two days' pay for each day they were on strike. Since the strike lasted from September to November, we didn't receive a paycheck until February of the following year.

All over the country, teachers' unions sympathetic to our cause tried to help us. Unfortunately, the police

were *not* sympathetic in the least. Whenever we pick-
eted, police motorcycles would "inadvertently" cross
the picket lines. Tires were slashed, obscene phone calls
made, families threatened. Some days I found myself
wondering wearily if working for the Mafia might have
been easier.

During those months, I spent my mornings picket-
ing, my afternoons at a bank where I stuffed and sealed
envelopes at minimum wage. I made just enough to buy
groceries.

By this time, my daughter Renee had finished college
and moved to Japan to teach English as a Second Language to businessmen there; she ended up marrying one
of them. Denise was just starting college, determined
to pursue a dance career, either on stage or as a dance
therapist. Only my youngest, Nicole, was left at home.
I felt very alone, terribly frightened that I would fail to
provide for her. At the time, my parents were estranged
from me over the divorce, and Pete's child support didn't
stretch far enough to cover a teenage girl's needs.

Then, in the midst of my anxiety, I began to experience a strange new sensation. It felt like a flame burned
in the center of my solar plexus, a mysterious fiery sensation of physical heat. I would find myself thinking: *The
world has existed for billions of years, and billions of
human beings have come and gone. Life is so full. Who
knows what lies beyond it? Why should I be concerned
about something as trivial as a school strike, as fleeting as
finances?*

This experience of internal fire occurred off and on throughout the months we were on strike. I told no one about it. I didn't know how to put it into words, even to myself. Strangely, however, I knew it helped me maintain the strength I needed.

From time to time, I wondered vaguely if this weren't the stirrings of that hidden something that had made me happy so long ago: A song? A voice? Something familiar and beloved?

Hogwash, I told myself when these thoughts came. *I'm done with all that.* I had learned long ago not to confuse my imagination with spiritual reality, I reminded myself. A spiritual revolution was already burning its way through my heart, but I still hadn't let myself recognize what was happening to me. Instead, I told myself I wasn't about to go *that* route again.

As the months passed and the strike ended, my life took on a new semblance of normalcy. As unobtrusively as it began, the inner flame faded away. I grew used to being on my own, without my husband. Still, I was hungry for something, though I hadn't the faintest what it was or how I should pursue it.

Should I go to school?

No, that didn't seem quite what I needed.

Go to conferences and workshops?

Maybe.

7

Leave the familiar for a while.
Greet yourself
as you mount the hidden tide
and travel back home.
Hafiz

The first workshop I attended was on mythology and primitive religions, taught by Joseph Campbell and Joan Halifax at Columbia University. I enjoyed it so much that I decided to attend as many of these as I could. Something about the material resonated with the vague stirrings within my mind and spirit. It amplified them, made them easier to hear. My old longing wrapped itself around the new knowledge, and together they called me to go further, deeper.

During this time, I also discovered the Theosophical Society. Madam Blavatsky, the first Russian woman to be naturalized as an American citizen, and Henry S. Olcott, an American colonel, established the society back in 1897. As a young woman, Madam Blavatsky had traveled all over the world searching for wisdom about the nature of life and the reason for human existence. She brought both the spiritual wisdom of the East and the ancient Western mysteries to the modern West at a time when they were virtually unknown to most Americans. Her synthesis of religious ideas—which eventually became known as Theosophy—sought to remove religious antagonism and draw together people of good will whatever their religion. The union Theosophy encouraged was not the profession of a common belief, Madam Blavatsky said, but instead a shared search and aspiration for Truth.

By the 1970s, her society was headquartered in India, with offices in New York City. I visited these and became totally absorbed in the new perspectives on the spiritual realm that the society offered. I discovered that the great father of Roman Catholic theology, Thomas Aquinas, didn't have all the answers; Greek philosophy was not the only foundation for truth; Buddha didn't get it wrong; and Krishna could compete with some of Christianity's best revelations! Intellectually, I was having fun, playing with new ideas.

Emotionally, I was a wreck. I had discovered the heady joy of theological ideas—but ideas alone had no power to heal the pain within me.

A teacher recommended I go to a Jungian analyst for help, and I was desperate enough to take her advice. (I never saw the teacher again; looking back, I am struck by the strange way in which people pop in and out of our lives, often leaving us with lasting gifts, the very things we needed most.)

Jungian therapy, I discovered, is unlike other talk therapies. Its long and complex methods include dream analysis, automatic writing, creative imagination, the study of archetypes, and other esoteric techniques. Recognizing the divinity that resides within us, Jung combined spirituality with psychoanalysis. He referred to this combination of psyche and spirit as the Self, something, he said, which was different from the ego self, that outer shell of personality we think of ourselves as being.

Dr. Gertrud Ujhely, my new analyst, was a short, plump woman who had been born in Vienna, then fled the Nazis and trained for many years in the United States. When I first met her, we shook hands, and the grip of her fingers held a formidable strength. I immediately knew I was safe.

During our sessions, I sat in a large rust-colored chair in her office. Cherry bookshelves lined the room from floor to ceiling, each book placed neatly according to its subject matter. The floor was oak, with a couple of gold rugs scattered across it. Her desk faced a wide window that overlooked a garden lush with flowering bushes and trees. I felt a sense of calm energy contained within the room.

Over the next fourteen years, I went to Gertrud for both long and short stretches. Today, although Gertrud is long gone, I still remember her office as a place of both safety and challenge, and I continue to hold her in my heart. Her guidance was a pivot point in my life.

As I worked with her, she tried to teach me something I had never suspected: God had been there, inside me, all along. And if God was there—if God was my Self, in some way I still didn't understand—how could I hate myself the way I had throughout my entire life? All these years, had I been silencing *God's* voice within me? This new thought gripped me with a sense of amazed and incredulous awe—but it was just a thought. I played with it intellectually like a delightful new toy—but I failed to grasp it with my heart.

At one point, Gertrud told me to pick up the Bible and read the story of the beheading of John the Baptist. I knew the story well; after all, I'd gone to a Catholic school, and I'd seen the incident portrayed in movies as well. I couldn't guess what she thought I'd learn from this bloody story.

"Marietta," she said in her thick Viennese accent, "everyone has archetypes at work in their lives. You must discover yours to better understand your life. It is difficult to explain, this role of archetypes in our lives, but they are very ancient human patterns. Jung believed that by understanding them we gain a deeper understanding of our Self."

So I read the story again, and then again. And again and again. And finally, suddenly, it came to me: Herod was my father, Herod's wife was my mother, and Salome was me. The dynamic among the three of us was the same dance of perverted power.

At the next session I begged her to tell me more.

"Ah, Marietta," she said, "I shouldn't have to explain what is only too obvious. Here you were, an innocent child who loved life. Salome, too, loved life and she loved to dance—but she had a controlling mother who could easily force Salome to do her bidding, regardless of how horrific it was. Too terrified to do otherwise, Salome would consent. Sound familiar, eh?"

I nodded.

"And then there was Herod, the father figure, who was not only afraid to go against what others thought, but who also lusted after this young girl. He thought to own her, to control her as though she were an extension of himself rather than a separate individual. He told her he'd give her anything she wanted, if only she'd dance for him and his guests. Right?"

I shifted uneasily in my seat, remembering the way my father had once placed me on my grandmother's table and made me sing.

"Salome," Gertrud continued, "not knowing what to ask for—for when others control us, we often lose the ability to hear our own desires—ran to her mother. The mother knew exactly what *she* wanted. She used her daughter to achieve her own desires. Once again, the daughter was forced to be an extension of the parents, a means for them to achieve their own unhealthy desires. This strange capsule of events contains your archetype, Marietta."

"And John the Baptist?" I asked her. "Who is he in my life?"

"What do you think?"

At first, all I could come up with was the word *sac-rifice.* John had given up his life; he became the scape-goat—and so had I. So was I both Salome *and* John in this story?

I read the story again—and then it hit me! Salome was my ego self, but John was the greater Self within me. Scripture called John a "voice crying in the wilderness"; he had been killed, sacrificed, so that his voice could no longer be heard. Salome's mother had seen to it that his voice was silenced forever—just as my voice had been silenced.

I needed time to take it all in. I mulled over it. I wrote a play about it. Some of Gertrud's analysis seemed right to me, but other parts made me uncomfortable. Surely my father had never felt the way Gertrud said Herod had toward Salome. He hadn't *lusted* after me.

Then I thought of my father's rage long ago when he saw me kissing the young man good night. I remembered how he had intruded even on my honeymoon. I realized that despite his disapproval, he had also seemed oddly pleased when Pete and I divorced. I remembered count-less incidents where he'd acted toward me with a strange possessiveness. *As though he'd owned me.*

✳✳✳

Jungian therapy is not meant to be short or easy. It cer-tainly wasn't in my case. A time came when Gertrud and

I reached an impasse. An impasse, she told me, happens when the unconscious mind refuses to reveal more material because it's too frightened; the repressed material is too overwhelming.

I felt as if something inside me had frozen. My sessions with Gertrud became sterile. I couldn't think of anything to talk about. My voice had once again fallen silent, and I could no longer access the place from which it spoke.

Gertrud decided to try another tactic. Jung had included astrology in his overall study of the human psyche, so she recommended a Jungian astrologer to help me. I was surprised and a little reluctant, but despite everything, something inside me had become endlessly, stubbornly hopeful.

Jungian astrology studies the movements and nuances of the human psyche with serious intelligence. It's a far cry from the penny-ante foolishness common in newspapers and websites, and yet most people don't know the difference between the two. I'm still not completely sure what I think about it, but I believe that somehow this pseudoscience arrives at truth through nonlinear, irrational, and illogical methods.

Most of us modern-day Westerners, however, are devout believers in the Scientific Method; anything else seems like nonsense. Consequently, at the time, I felt a little embarrassed to seek out the help of an astrologer, no matter how intellectual and intelligent she might be. I found myself thinking of a Jesuit priest, though, who had proudly announced to our class in his Irish brogue, "There's a teeny bit of truth in everything, me darlin's." I decided to give this astrologer a try.

To reach her tiny cottage on the eastern end of Long Island, close to the Sound, I had to drive down winding dirt roads. When I finally arrived, the cottage was so picturesque and tiny that I half-expected Hansel and Gretel to come prancing out.

Instead, a robust woman with white hair greeted me at the door. Her smile was warm, tinged with a bit of mischief. She led me into the living room and then left me while she went into the kitchen to brew some tea.

I looked around me. Shelves holding papers, pictures, charts, and books lined the walls. White lace curtains framed a large window that looked out into the woods. I caught a glimpse of a tiny dining area and stairs that led up to a loft.

She came back with our tea, and we immediately got to work. After reading my astrological chart, she leaned back and looked at me. Like a fairy godmother handing me a secret treasure, she announced, "Your path, my girl, is a mystical one. If I were you, I'd pursue it. Furthermore, I'd connect with the Sufis. Their path is not only mystical but strewn with music, dancing, and poetry. You'll like it. They will teach the creative side of you. You know you're deeply creative, don't you?"

I gulped. Part of me wanted to scream with joy, *Yes!* At the same time, I had no idea what she was talking about. I had never heard of people known as Sufis.

Suddenly, all I wanted to do was run away. I paid her, thanked her, and left. *So much for that*, I thought to myself.

✳✳✳

In the meantime, while all this was going on, I went about my life. I was teaching, mothering, shopping, doing all the normal things a working parent does.

Then one afternoon, a colleague of mine told me about a group to which he belonged that followed the teachings of G. I. Gurdjieff, an Armenian spiritual leader and mystic. These teachings were known as The Work, my colleague told me. He invited me to join him at one of the group's meetings.

It was held in a run-down, four-story house on the top of a hill overlooking the Long Island Sound. One of Gurdjieff's first students, a woman named Mrs. Popoff who was said to have once married a Russian Count, owned the house. When she welcomed newcomers like me, she always told the same story.

"I was eighteen and anxious to study with Gurdjieff," she would say, "so I arranged a meeting with him in the middle of Manhattan. I never thought he'd consent to meet with me—but he did. He was of medium height with dark hair and very dark eyes that penetrated my being. This was a man who could not be touched by coyness or diplomacy. Even then he was a Master.

"We sat down at a table and he asked me what I would like to drink. I courteously replied, 'I'll have whatever you have.'

"He turned to the waiter and said, 'We'll have two triple brandies.'

"I was not much of a drinker, and I tried unsuccessfully to stifle my gasp. He grinned at me.

"'Always know what you want!' he advised me."

I did not know what I wanted, though, and so I was in much the same situation Mrs. Popoff had been: I was about to be served something that was far more than I had intended—and not quite to my taste.

The weekly meetings with Mrs. Popoff consisted of classes first and then cleanup. This meant cleaning the four floors of her house (which also housed a large number of cats, twenty or so). *Pretty smart*, I thought to myself. *Get your disciples to clean your house each week and you won't need a cleaning lady.*

But no, I was told, this was also part of the spiritual teaching, a way to practice consciousness while working.

I held out for as long as I could. Then one night, as I was sweeping the kitchen floor, one of Mrs. Popoff's disciples confronted me. "You're not doing it right."

I wasn't sure I'd understood her. "What did you say?"

"I said," she annunciated carefully, as though I might be hard of hearing, "you're not sweeping the kitchen floor correctly."

I'd been sweeping kitchen floors for forty or so years, and I was pretty sure I knew how to do it. "Look," I said, "if you have something to tell me, don't beat around the bush."

"You're not doing this right, because you're not doing it consciously," the woman snapped. "We work consciously here, or we don't work at all."

"How do you know I'm not doing this consciously? Can you read my mind?" But I barely heard her answer. The odor of cat urine that permeated the air was suddenly too much for me. I'd had enough! This wasn't for me.

Over the years since then I've come to admire Gurdjieff's teachings. The movie *Meetings with Remarkable Men* gives a beautiful synopsis of his life and work, and his influence over those who pursue the spiritual life continues to be real and significant. But I wasn't ready for it at that point in my life.

But that damned word—*Sufi*—had been haunting me ever since the astrologer had pronounced it. Finally, one afternoon I picked up the phonebook and flipped to the S's.

The Sufis, I discovered, had a center on 14th Street in lower Manhattan, one of the dreariest parts of the city.

I decided to give them a try.

8

Sufism is not rituals and forms,
and it is not bodies of knowledge,
not doctrines, not ideas, not theories.
It is simply the way a lover is
in the presence of the Beloved.
Abu'l-Hasan al-Nuri

The Sufi Order was located in an eighteenth-century corner building in the midst of a neighborhood that was a haven for drug addicts, alcoholics, and homeless people. I stood outside the building and looked around me. *God seems to like hanging out in the damnedest places,* I found myself thinking.

But I wasn't looking for God, I told myself. I wasn't seeking a mystical way either, so I wasn't altogether sure what I was doing there. All I knew was that I'd taken many twists and turns on my journey toward transformation, toward truth, toward whatever it was that I *was* seeking. So far, I hadn't found the answer. I might as well try one more thing.

The Order occupied the top floor of the building. The space consisted of a chapel, a large kitchen and dining room, an office, several bedrooms, and one bathroom. A few Sufis lived there, but most lived in apartments elsewhere in the city. Classes, Sufi dancing, liturgy, and the practice of zikr were held at this Manhattan center. The main center, however, was situated on hundreds of acres of land upstate in New Lebanon, New York.

But on that afternoon, as I stepped out of the elevator into the Sufi quarters, I still knew none of this. I was anxious and curious, but I didn't have a clue what to expect.

The first thing I noticed was a large black-and-white photograph of a man dressed in Middle Eastern garb. He had a long beard, penetrating eyes, and stature that was straight and dignified, yet I sensed something gentle about him.

While I was still studying his face, a door opened and a woman came out. Her glossy black hair, her beauty, her entire demeanor was somehow daunting. I instantly felt thrown back upon myself, the feeling you get when something unexpected but exquisite takes you by surprise and you are immediately humbled. She smiled then and took my hand to usher me into her office.

Her voice was quiet as she asked me about my life, and I relaxed. Her attention never waivered while I spoke, and I found myself feeling totally accepted. As she began to answer my questions, I sensed I was entering a strange new world, one that would either repel or delight me. In either case, I could not resist exploring further.

In a clear, firm voice that somehow managed to be also soothing, she said, "No one knows the origin of Sufism. Legend has it that around the fourth century men wearing wool—*suf* means wool—roamed the deserts of the Middle East, searching for a life with God. These wanderers organized themselves around Islam, adopting many of its precepts and culture. They came to be known as Islamic mystics."

"Then Sufis are Muslims?" I asked.

She shook her head. "A Sufi can belong to any religion, because Sufism is not a religion, it is a spiritual path. There are many Jews, Christians, and Hindus who are also Sufis. One does not negate the other. If you are a Christian, you can attend church, receive the sacraments, and so on—and still walk the Sufi path. In fact, before the fourth century—before Sufis attached themselves to Islam—legend has it that many Sufis followed Jesus."

"How do they think of God then?" I was trying to lay this new slant on Christianity over the one I had always known, but I was finding it difficult to see how they lined up. "I'm sure they don't think in terms of the Trinity as Christians do."

The woman shook her head again. "The Trinity is a dogma that Christians are asked to believe. Dogmas and doctrines are all part of the foundational theology of every religion. But since Sufism is not a religion, our 'dogma'—if we can even call it that—is one of love. God is referred to as the Beloved." She fell silent for a moment and then said, "The purpose of creation is revealed in these words: 'I was a Hidden Treasure, and I longed to be known, and so I created the world.'"

"That's beautiful." The words she had quoted rolled over me again and again, filling me with thoughts I had never experienced.

She nodded. "For us this is the ultimate truth. God wishes us to know Him, and He wishes to know Himself through us."

I frowned. "Wishes to know Himself? Surely, He knows Himself. He wouldn't be God if He didn't know Himself, would He?"

"Yes, and no." Her smile was kind, lacking any conde-scension. "If Sufism acknowledges one central truth it is that we are not separate from the Divine, nor have we ever been. And yet at the same time, we know that the Beloved is always the initiator: God loves us long before we love Him, He is pursuing us before we ever think to pursue Him. But we can recognize this only by unveiling our inner eye, that is, the eye of the heart, and seeing what we have not perceived before. Until this happens, we walk around blinded, mistaking what we see as real-ity. The life we build when we are in this state is nothing but a bed of straw. What we think has value is only an illusion."

I struggled to keep up with her, but it was all so new to me. Only later, would I go back and begin to understand all she was telling me.

"Seeing with the eye of the heart," she continued, "is not an emotional response to life. It is not about *feeling.*

Instead, it requires that we develop an intuitive sense that includes mind, heart, and body. Only when your spiritual senses are mature will you be able to hear the voice of the Beloved calling to you."

She continued to explain Sufism—and I continued to listen, piecing together this amazing new perspective on life, one that seemed too good to be believed. Despite the small cynical corner of my mind, I was eager to learn more.

"Sufis," the woman said, "consider union with God to be their lives' sole purpose."

Although Sufis believe in a transcendent God, I learned, they stress Divine immanence as well. They recognize the Beloved in everything, especially in human beings, a theological concept known as panentheism. Unlike pantheism, where the world *is* God, panentheism teaches that God is *in* all things. With pantheism, God is the whole, while according to panentheism, the whole is in God. If this is the case, then to be truly human is to be truly divine. Far from canceling out one another, our divinity is in direct proportion to our humanity.

"Throughout history," the woman continued, "Sufis have been persecuted for this belief. A Sufi might utter phrases such as, 'I am the Beloved!'—and for Muslims who believe God's transcendence is paramount, this notion is not only heretical but downright demonic." She smiled. "This is why Sufis often attempted to hide themselves, parading as madmen or drunkards. Their poetry was full of symbolism—wine, dance, song, erotic love—all used to cover their awareness of this divine truth. Their shenanigans didn't always protect them, of course—nor did they necessarily care about protection. Truth was their pearl of great price. It was more important to them than their lives."

She told me the stories of Sufi saints whose love for the Beloved was so extravagant that it cost them their lives, men like Abu Yazid al-Bastami who responded to a Muslim's cry of "Glory be to God!" with "Glory be to me!"—or Al Hallaj who went to his death exclaiming, "I am the truth!"

The woman smiled as she told these stories. "They sound like mad men, don't they? But really, they were no more scandalous than Jesus. In the same way he turned the world upside down, they were trying to break through the hard shell of legalism."

A question occurred to me. "Were they all men?"

"Of course not. Our greatest woman saint was Rabia, who lived in the eighth century. Legend has it that she received quite a few proposals of marriage, but she would always say, 'I'm not interested in having my attention distracted from God even for a split second.' She was known to keep all-night vigils, and she wrote poetry filled with descriptions of consummated love for her Beloved."

One day, I learned, a servant girl said to Rabia, "It's spring! Why not come outside and look at all the beauty God has made?"

To which Rabia replied, "Why not come inside instead? And see the One who made it all, naked without a veil."

By the time the woman stopped talking, I was nearly dizzy from so much new information. She seemed to sense my confusion. "We needn't go into this too deeply at this point. Perhaps I can show you some books that may be more to your understanding. One thing we do know—treading a path we've never tread before must be done slowly and consciously. In other words, one step at a time."

She brought me into a room with walls covered by shelves of books. I saw that most of them were written by Hazrat Inayat Khan, the man who first brought Sufism to the United States. (I learned that it was his picture that had greeted me at the elevator.) He was born in India, left for America as a young musician, and married an American woman. His eldest son, Pir Vilayat Khan, was now head of the Sufi Order. There are many Sufi orders, but this one was then known as the Sufi Order of the West. (It has since changed its name to the Sufi Order International.)

As she brought our meeting to a close, she recommended that I read a book called *The Alchemy of Happiness*, written by Inayat Khan. "And I hope you'll consider attending a zikr class on Thursday evening," she added.

"Zikr? What's that?"

"It's a spiritual practice, in fact the main spiritual practice of our order. You can come and observe if you wish.

You can even bring someone if that will make you feel more comfortable."

She embraced me, I thanked her, and then I left.

What in the name of heaven am I doing? I thought as I walked down the street. *Come back? At night, in this part of town? With drunks and addicts sleeping on the sidewalks? No way.*

But I decided to give the book a try.

＊＊＊

The book made sense. Each sentence was a call to compassion; each paragraph, a witness to love.

I called my brother on the phone. "Hey, Nicky, I know you'll think I'm as nuts as ever, but do you mind coming to this Sufi meeting with me? It's in downtown Manhattan, not in a good part of town. Frankly, I'm a bit nervous to go alone."

My brother agreed, and on Thursday evening, we rode the rickety elevator to the top floor of the Sufis' building. This time, when we stepped off the elevator, the place was filled with people, all waiting to be ushered into the chapel.

For the most part, they were a silent group, with a few smiles here and there as friends greeted each other. I shot nervous glances at them, thinking they all looked like ordinary New Yorkers, the same people you'd see on the subway. Nothing especially exotic or spiritual.

The chapel doors opened, and people took their places. Nicky and I, as newcomers who were unfamiliar with the practice, were directed to the back row of the circle. We took our seats, and I looked around.

The chapel shone with crystal and white: white linen on the altar, white roses in crystal vases, white candles in crystal holders, white rug, and white robes worn by the elder Sufis. All else was dark, save for the flickering light from seven candles on the altar. Clad in their long robes, the Sufis knelt in a circle. Slowly, they began the practice of zikr.

In unison, they rolled their heads from left to right, then bowed, heads touching the floor, and rose, looking down toward their hearts. As they made these movements, they uttered Arabic syllables: "*La ilaha illa-Allah Hu*"—"There is no god but God the Beloved." Specifically, the first part—"*La ilaha*"—means to wipe the slate clean; we are to go beyond all our beliefs, all our concepts. And then, "*illa-Allah*"—except for God—and finally, "*Hu*" (done while looking down toward the heart), which means not my knowledge of God, but God's own intimate and loving knowledge of God-Self through me. They repeated the zikr over and over. Sometimes the words were changed to "*Ishq Allah, Mabud Allah*," spoken more softly, which translates as "God is Lover and the Beloved."

The robed figures moved so slowly at first, slowly, slowly, then faster, then faster still, with greater and greater momentum, until their voices and feet reverberated like thunder within the room. The noise and movement created a state I later learned is known as "celestial hypnosis."

A part of me observed all this coolly from a distance, wondering if I was getting involved in some sort of exotic cult. Except for the absence of hoods, they could all be mistaken for members of the Ku Klux Klan. And yet another part of me was mesmerized by the sense of the sacred that permeated the room.

Afterward, as we left, I was acutely aware of a sense of lightness in my body.

"Well," my brother asked, "will you be coming back?"

"I'm not sure," I lied. I couldn't talk about it, nor could I explain what I was feeling. But I knew I'd return.

✳✳✳

Week after week, through rain, snow, ice, even sickness, I returned to the building in lower Manhattan. For the first time in my life, I was hearing something I had always longed to hear, though I'd never known what it was: that Divine love is so completely unconditional that God sees only our perfection.

Perfection? The very word seemed impossible in connection with my so very-imperfect self, and yet slowly, I came to understand that my innermost being is perfect; that the image of God is in me, and nothing can destroy or mar or limit it. Regardless of my sin—all my nonsense, depravity, cruelty, and pride—a place exists inside me that remains pure and whole, untouched by all I had experienced in life.

These ideas were all so new to me then, but later I would read a better description of what I was coming to understand, one written by the Catholic mystic Thomas Merton:

> *At the center of our being is a point of nothingness which is untouched by sin and by illusion, a point of pure truth, a point of spark which belongs entirely to God, which is never at our disposal, from which God disposes our lives, which is inaccessible to the fantasies of our own mind or the brutalities of our own will. This little point of nothingness and of absolute poverty is the pure glory of God in us . . . it is in everybody, and if we could see it we would see these billions of points coming together in the face and blaze of a sun that would make all the darkness and cruelty of life vanish completely.*

At the time, it was simply too much for me to take in all at once. My new understanding kept getting mixed up with the God of my childhood, and Catholicism still seemed to me to be "real" religion. *After all,* I would find myself thinking, *the Sufis aren't Catholic, so they're probably too simplistic in their beliefs.* Unconditional Divine love seemed too good to be true, a way to justify getting away with anything. Go ahead and sin! Have a ball! God will love you anyway! I was irresistibly drawn to what I was learning from the Sufis, but at the same time, I insisted upon taking everything with a grain of salt.

Sufism is a well-established belief system, though, one that is deeply and carefully rooted. I learned that Sufis are under the tutelage of sheiks or masters, people who have reached high levels of consciousness, whose roles are to keep each Sufi on the right path. In the Middle East, this relationship continues as it did in centuries past, but here in the West, most Sufi initiates depend on a spiritual guide for instruction, while a sheik is available to oversee them and give them the teachings of the Order.

Without these relationships, Sufis believe we are subject to distractions and illusions that interfere with spiritual growth. A well-known adage is, "A Sufi without a sheik has Satan for his sheik." The disciple places herself entirely in the master's hands and becomes "like a corpse in the hands of the body-washer." The goal of this submission is the total effacement of the ego, the psychic death that signals the true birth of the spiritual life. I felt both curious and wary as I learned about this aspect of Sufism.

One night a Sufi sheik named Shahabbadin came to the Manhattan center, a jolly, rotund man who had once been a New York lawyer. His practice had made his Jewish parents proud, but he had renounced it all when he became a Sufi. On this particular night, he was initiating people into the Order and giving them their Sufi names.

Names, the Sufis believe, reveal a person's unique individual essence. By hearing your name spoken over and over in reference to yourself, your unconscious is activated into eliciting the quality the name represents—and this in turn helps us manifest God on Earth more fully. Our true names lead us to God; and then the Divine is revealed through our own identities. The Beloved wishes to experience this life through us and as us.

Again, these ideas seemed so strange and new to me, so different from what the Catholic Church had taught me. And yet eventually I learned these ideas are buried within Christianity's heart as well. Teresa of Avila, the sixteenth-century mystic recognized as a Doctor of the Church, expressed a very similar concept:

> *Christ has no body now but yours. No hands, no feet on earth but yours. Yours are the eyes through which He looks compassion on this world. Christ has no body now on earth but yours.*

On that evening of initiation, however, I was only a moth caught in the light, fluttering in fascinated circles around something I still could not understand. And then, Shahabaddin looked around the room, and his eyes met mine.

"Would you like to be initiated into the Order?"

"Oh, no!" I blurted, taken by surprise. "I'm not ready."

"Why don't you let me be the judge of that?" He smiled. "What's your name?"

"Marietta."

"Well, Marietta, you needn't be afraid. I believe you *are* ready. There's no commitment for you to make tonight that you haven't already made in your heart."

Oh yeah? How do you know? I wondered, but I let him lead me to the altar. He placed his hand on my head and spoke a few words. Then he said, "Salima. This is to be your name. It means peaceful sage."

I bowed my head—and all the while, I was thinking, *Boy, are you off track!* Me? Peaceful? A sage? I tried to keep my skepticism from showing on my face.

Then I remembered that the Sufi name is given to call forth a certain quality. So, I reasoned, perhaps Shahabaddin had looked into the tumult and confusion within me and wished me to be more at peace.

"One more thing," he said. "You would do well to find yourself a spiritual guide, one who can see your heart." He smiled, embraced and blessed me, and then left the room.

✳✳✳

In the months that followed, I grew accustomed to being called by my new name. I wasn't especially looking for a spiritual guide during this time, but then one day, while I was attending a workshop at the Sufi center, I noticed a young woman. She was smiling down at me from a flight of stairs, and though I didn't recall ever being introduced to her, she knew my name. "Hi, Salima," she called to me.

I looked up at her smile. Something inside me that had been closed for years opened, and I knew she was the guide I needed.

Her name was Blanchefleur ("white flower" in French), a name that fit her well; although she was ten years younger than I, her hair was a dazzling white. At that point, she had been in the Order about eleven years. I learned she was married and had three little boys. Taj, the wife of Pir Vilayat, the head of the Sufi Order, was a good friend of hers. All that information was incidental, though; I knew the important thing about her was her smile. Somehow, that smile told me I could trust her.

Our first meeting for spiritual direction was not what I had expected. We sat on the floor opposite each other, our eyes closed, saying nothing. The silence seemed to last an eternity.

Finally, she opened her eyes. "You don't realize how much you are loved."

The tears I had held back for years streamed down my face. I don't remember much else except driving home that night, feeling as if the car were flying off the ground. I was an adult woman with grown daughters, but at that moment I felt more like the thirteen-year-old who was absolutely certain that the Blessed Mother had smiled at her.

9

Our names are but names for God;
at the same time our individual selves are His shadow.
He is you and not you, all at the same time.
Think about that!

Ibn 'Arabi

A year went by before I personally met the head of the Order, Pir Vilayat. He was conducting a seminar at Columbia University, and Blanchefleur wanted me to meet him.

After her introduction, she said to him, "Perhaps, Pir Vilayat, you can give Salima a new name?"

I had not expected this, but I said nothing. I was learning to submit to my Sufi guide's leading.

"Yes," he responded. "Salima is not quite right." Then he turned and left.

Throughout the rest of the conference, I waited for Pir Vilayat to tell me my new name. Then the conference was over, and he was gone. I was terribly disappointed, but Blanchefleur reassured me. "You'll get your new name when the time is right."

Another year passed, and then once more Pir Vilayat was at Columbia for a seminar; and once more I attended. I was convinced he would have forgotten about me by this time. After all, he met so many people, traveling all over the world giving conferences, meeting with other Sufi leaders. But during the seminar break, Blanchefleur came over to me and said, "Why don't you go backstage and ask him about your name?"

I shook my head. "He'd never remember me. He met me only once over a year ago."

She shrugged. "Give it a try anyhow."

Sheepishly, shyly, I tiptoed backstage and peeked through the curtain. Pir Vilayat was pacing back and forth, his eyes on the floor, apparently deep in thought. With his snowy white beard, white hair, and long white robe he looked like an apparition, some unworldly and intimidating sage. Still, my spiritual guide had told me to approach him, and it was my job to obey her.

"Pir Vilayat?" I squeaked.

He looked up at me. "Oh, yes." He nodded. "I have just the name for you." He spoke as though we were continuing a conversation that had been only briefly interrupted. "My sense is that you've suffered a great deal with regard to your creativity. Yes, a great deal. And so I've given you the name Bahri." He spelled it for me, and then added, "It means creativity—but always include that little breath of air for the 'h.' Never leave it out. I have put it there to indicate that yours is the creativity that creates from something that is already there, not from nothing, as

God does. It is God working through you. Remember that too."

"Yes, I will." I was shaking, but a sense of calm settled within me.

He took my hand in his and blessed me, then resumed his pacing.

I scurried to find Blanchefleur. "Did you tell Pir Vilayat about my life?" I demanded. She was the only one in the Order who knew my story, so no one else could have told him.

She smiled and shook her head. "No, not a word."

I thought of the way my singing voice had disappeared. I thought of my dreams of the theatre. I thought of everything I had lost over the years. And I was flooded with a new sense of possibility, a glimpse of the long-ago little girl who had sung with joy.

In my mind, I went over Pir Vilayat's words again and again, studying them. "Do you understand what he meant about the 'h' in my new name?" I asked Blanchefleur. "When I looked up *bahri* in an Arabic dictionary, it meant something different."

She thought a moment, then said slowly, "'Bari' is one of the ninety-nine names of Allah. It means the Creator, and it is a *wazifa*." By this time, I knew a wazifa was a word or syllable we recited over and over, meditating on it, allowing it to evoke Divine qualities in our hearts. "So by putting the 'h' in this word," Blanchefleur continued, "Pir has made your name different from the wazifa. He allowed the breath of the Beloved to enter it, so that you would remember it is God breathing creation through you."

I attended the rest of the conference, but I couldn't absorb anything more. I was stunned, confused, and nearly giddy with happiness. I loved my new name. When it was spoken, something deep within me resonated with it. For the first time in my life, I felt completely understood.

✳✳✳

The Sufis offered me a freedom and acceptance I had never before experienced. I thrived under their influence. My life now consisted of weekly meetings, Sunday liturgy, frequent seminars, and countless hours spent immersed in books by the Sufi masters.

One of these, Abu Muhammad Muta'ish, had written:

> *The Sufi is he whose thought keeps pace with his foot, in other words, he is entirely present: his soul is where his body is, and his body where his soul is, and his soul where his foot is, and his foot where his soul is. This is the sign of presence without absence. Others say on the contrary: "He is absent from himself but present with God." It is not so: he is present with himself and present with God.*

As I took part in the Sufis' spiritual practices, I gained a new way to think about both myself and God. I was learning to be present to both myself and the One the Sufis called the Beloved.

Besides the practice of zikr, we had a liturgy created to honor every major religion. Referred to as the Universal Worship service, it included all the sacred scriptures from all the major religions, each placed on the altar. On the left side were the scriptures from Hinduism, Buddhism, and Zoroastrianism. On the right were Judaism, Christianity, and Islam. A Sufi text at the center of the altar separated East from West. A theme was chosen for each service and appropriate texts read from the various scriptures, illustrating that all religions echo the deepest truths. A sermon followed, and the service ended with all participating in a Sufi dance.

Dance is the spiritual practice that many people connect with Sufism, since it's been made famous by the "whirling dervishes." It involves a spinning motion upon the axis of a perfectly upright body, arms stretched on either side, the right palm upward to receive the graces of heaven, and the left palm downward to pass them on to the Earth. While maintaining the motion on the body's axis, everyone in the group moves around a circle, like planets around the sun. As they whirl, worshipers also meditate. Some people go into ecstasy.

Another Sufi practice is the wazifa, repeating specific vocal sounds in order to call forth a divine quality that is attempting to come through us. These ancient sounds have been practiced for centuries. Almost primitive in tone, they're believed to elicit the specific divine qualities we need.

Busy as we are with worries and fears about both the past and the future, humans often miss the opportunities they have to hear what God has to say. Rumi, perhaps the greatest of the Sufi poets, wrote: "Each moment contains a hundred messages from God. To every cry of 'Oh Lord,' He answers a hundred times, 'I am here.'" I was finally learning to listen to a voice I had nearly forgotten existed.

***

That same year, I attended another conference at Columbia University. The day was one of those magical autumn days in New York, saturated with the red and gold of fallen leaves, while the wind blew against us like an unruly child, knocking off hats and pushing us toward our destinations.

During the noon break, I decided to have lunch outside a café a few blocks from Columbia. As I sat there, I noticed that the intense blue of the sky overhead was the same shade as the blue I once wore as a schoolgirl in honor of the Virgin Mary. As that random thought entered my mind, I was suddenly, powerfully, catapulted back to the memory of those long-ago mornings when I walked beneath the trees on my way to Mass, praying to Mary that she would bring me back if I ever strayed.

And she had. She hadn't used the Church to do it, though. Instead, she had used Sufism. She had once more smiled at me, but this time through Blanchefleur, through all I had learned, through all I had come to love.

Mary had never been angry with me, I realized. She had never rejected me. Her love had been with me through it all—and she had given me the capacity now to hear the voice of love.

The Beloved was calling to me with a voice I had thought I would never hear again.

10

The body is like Mary
and each of us has a Jesus inside.
We are all in holy labor,
working to deliver God.
When we are caught up in the earth's loveliness,
in our own soul's capacity for beauty,
then we know, if only for a moment,
without doubts,
that God is really there within us. . .
needing to be born.
He is breathed to life in our world
with our hands
and with our song.
Rumi

A few months after Pir Vilayat gave me my name, Blanchefleur told me she thought I should go on a retreat, a time of intense spiritual withdrawal from the world. I was familiar with the Catholic concept of retreats, but the last one I had done had been back in high school; that one, lead by a Franciscan, was such an intense experience that afterward I was ready to die and go to heaven. (*Why stick around?* I remember thinking. I wasn't exactly a happy camper at that point in my life.) With that memory still lingering in my mind, the thought of making another retreat after all this time intrigued me. What I didn't know was that a Sufi retreat was nothing like the Catholic version.

I arrived in New Lebanon, New York, the Sufi order's home base, with my suitcase in hand. I greeted the man who met me, and then he asked me to follow him to the place where I would be staying.

We climbed a steep hill through the trees. The snow was a few inches deep, and I felt as if I were in training to become a mountain climber. We reached the top at last, and my guide opened the door of a tiny hut. It was not much bigger than a doghouse.

The snowy hilltop was very quiet, with no other huts in view, though I could see an outhouse at a distance through the trees. "We built the huts with plenty of room between each one," the man told me, "so that each person can have complete solitude while on retreat."

Solitude? I looked around me. The sun was sinking, casting long shadows through the trees, and soon it would be dark. And here I would be all night, with no electricity and no water, except from a half-frozen stream we had passed on our climb. No one within the sound of my voice, not a living creature, except for birds and maybe an occasional deer. (I didn't dare ask if there were bears.) I wanted to run down the hill, get in my car, and drive home.

Instead, I looked inside the hut. I saw a cot, a small table with a kerosene lamp and a cassette player on it, and a tiny kerosene heater.

The man handed me a basket. "This has food and drink for your breakfast and lunch tomorrow. Your retreat guide will place your dinner outside the hut tomorrow evening. When she arrives, do not speak to her. You may write down any questions you have for her. She will tell you what practices to do, what tapes to listen to, and what prayers you need to say."

Apparently, my retreat guide would be able to discern all this simply by reading my questions and then looking at me, since I could not speak to her.

"Take walks as much as you like," the man concluded. "Sleep whenever your body is tired."

My body may have been tired—but I didn't at all sleep that night.

The next morning things looked brighter. The snow sparkled in the sunlight, and the trees glistened in the cold air. I listened to the birds calling in the trees, and I didn't even miss my usual three cups of morning coffee.

My diet while on retreat, I discovered, consisted of tofu, fresh fruits and vegetables, fruit juice, decaffeinated tea, and peanut butter. My retreat guide told me later that day that this type of diet would make me more sensitive to the spiritual energies at work within me.

The retreat was structured to facilitate transformation, in much the same way that the ancient alchemists carried out various procedures to transform lead to gold.

Each step of the retreat was designed to lead me deeper into the process, with a period of intense purification at the beginning. These were followed by more practices and prayers structured to create a gradual ascent into higher levels of consciousness. At the end of the retreat, other practices would guide me back into normal awareness.

Some of these practices were wazifas. Normally, Sufi guides give their disciples particular wazifas to do eleven times a day, but during a retreat, the retreat guide assigns specific wazifas to facilitate the process of transformation. While on retreat, I spent the bulk of my day with zikr and wazifas. The rest of the time, I listened to tapes of music and Pir Vilayat speaking, took walks, and prayed.

By about four o'clock on my first full day there, the lack of sleep, the solitude, the practices, and the special diet had all combined to do their job. I didn't feel particularly spiritual, however; I felt confused and strangely fearful. I told myself these feelings were all part of the purification process, that negative feelings needed to rise to the surface in order to be released. My rationalization didn't help me much.

Outside my hut, night was falling again. The snow-draped trees had been lovely in the sunshine; now their silent shrouded shapes seemed ominous. I sensed something hidden in the dark shadows, watching me, though I knew it was only my imagination. Soon, I reminded myself, my guide would be coming with my dinner. I hoped she would have something to say to me; I longed to see a human face, hear another voice beside my own.

In the meantime, I decided to draw the blinds and continue with the practices. To keep me company, I put a tape into the battery-run recorder and hit the play button.

The lively music shifted my mood almost immediately—and it took my consciousness along with it. I found myself filled with playful energy, out in the snow, throwing snowballs. Someone was there with me, tossing snowballs back at me. We shouted and giggled, fell together in a heap in the snow, then picked ourselves up, and started over again. Gasping with laughter, I took a step back to see who my companion was. And then my breath caught in my throat.

I was looking into Mary's face.

I knew who she was without a doubt, though I had always imagined her to be dignified, gentle, and regal, rather than noisy, high-spirited, and playful. But here she was, and I realized I wasn't the least bit uncomfortable. Oddly, it didn't seem strange to me that Mary would choose to join me in the middle of the dark woods for a snowball fight. I remember thinking, *Where else would she possibly want to be?*

And then the music stopped, and I found myself back in the hut. I sucked in a breath and looked around the tiny bare room. "What was *that?*" I asked myself, my voice loud in the silence. Was lack of sleep making me imagine things? Was this some sort of altered state of consciousness?

Was it real?

That night I slept soundly. I woke up feeling unusually calm and at peace. The entire day was filled with a joy that was nearly painful, an excruciating happiness.

When I returned home, I told Blanchefleur about the retreat. "What do you think?"

She smiled. "Your experience of Mary was valid. Never doubt it."

"But was it a vision? Or just my imagination?"

She shook her head. "It makes no difference."

✳✳✳

A year later, I went on another retreat. The format was the same, but my fears were greater. Knowing what to expect did not help me to feel better; in fact, just the opposite. I entered into the retreat with a sense of dread and reluctance.

And then, about midway into the retreat, Mary came to me again. This time she was inside the hut with me, standing silently with one hand resting on an enormous glowing globe that filled the entire room. I blinked at the sudden bright light—and then she was gone.

I sat on my cot and felt peace flow into me once again. She had been showing me her Son, I realized, that great Light that was bigger than she was.

✳✳✳

As I immersed myself in Sufism, Mary continued to haunt me. The next time I saw her, I was halfway through an intensive, ten-day retreat. I had finished the purification processes (and I suppose my consciousness had been altered somewhat in the process), when I looked across the table—and there she was, sitting in a chair with a sewing basket on the table beside her. She was sewing something that lay in her lap.

Here is the mother of God, I thought to myself, *and she's doing the most ordinary thing. How extraordinary!*

She looked up and smiled at me—and I realized I was being asked to rethink the way I looked at the spiritual life. I loved the unconventional, the esoteric, and yes, even at times, the bizarre. But the Divine One is to be found in the ordinary, the mundane, the everyday tasks. Whether we realize it or not, whether we like it or not, God is found there besides us, within us, in the midst of daily life.

✳✳✳

When I speak of these visits from Mary, I need to clarify what I'm saying. Even at the time, I knew that these "appearances" were not taking place in the ordinary physical realm. I did not "see" her with my physical eyes so much as my mental ones. However, these experiences were different from mere flights of imagination. They were sharper, more intense, and more *real*.

But the validity of experiences like this can be judged only by their fruits. What consequences do these events have? If they fill us with pride . . . or fear . . . or hatred for others, then we should be very careful about how we think about them. We should certainly discuss them with someone we trust to help us determine what steps we need to take. (Do we need to spend time in prayer? Do we need to seek counseling? Do we even, perhaps, need medical help?) On the other hand, we may experience something quite different: a greater sense of peace; a quiet joy that seems to follow us around; a longing to reach out to others; an increased concern for the entire world, including the animals and the Earth itself; a greater diligence in prayer; and a sense that our entire perspective has shifted, that we are now living more in the spiritual realm than we ever have before.

We may not immediately recognize the fruits of these experiences; they may remain hidden at first and be recognized only with hindsight, but they can never be taken from us. As the years go by and life presents us with its unforeseeable dilemmas, these mystical experiences are likely to sink down into unconsciousness. We may even forget all about them.

And that's as it should be. When all is said and done, we're not meant to pay all that much attention to spiritual experiences such as these. We certainly shouldn't spend any time talking about them or bragging about them. (If we do, we're likely to be considered odd—or psychotic!) These experiences don't render us holier than the next guy, nor do they mean that God loves us more than the person who never experiences anything remotely like them. They are gifts from God—but God gives many gifts, and the small daily ones—like the morning sun on our face or a friend's voice—are just as valuable if not more valuable than gifts that from our perspective seem so much more sensational. God gives us each what we need most at the place where we're at in our journey. Down the road, gifts that seemed so enormous at the time may seem far less important. What remains is the sweetness of infinite Love.

But I had yet to learn these lessons. Spiritual glutton that I had become, I wanted more. Weekly meetings, readings, spiritual practices, retreats, and teachings weren't enough. The sense of longing inside me pulled me forward, as though I were out on a lake on water skis, attached to a boat that was pulling me further and further from shore. Nothing else mattered to me now. Nothing was as important to me.

And so I took a leave of absence from teaching and sold my house. And then I moved to the Abode of the Message, the Sufi headquarters in New Lebanon.

11

A Sufi is thankful
not only for what he has been given
but also for all that has been denied.
Elif Shafak

Within hours of my arrival, I knew I had made a mistake, but I shoved the feeling deep inside, so deep that it didn't have a chance to resurface again until months later. I told myself I would soon settle in and feel at home. After all, I had been to the Abode many times by now, for retreats, conferences, and classes. This was a familiar place, the place where I must surely belong.

The Abode's central buildings, once part of a Shaker community, were at the center of the campus, while private homes for families with children were clustered around them. In the main buildings were housed a school, a huge kitchen, a dining hall, conference rooms, and a chapel. The rest of the old Shaker buildings were used for living space.

This was where I lived, in a room just large enough for a bureau, a dresser, a desk, and a bed. The floor-to-ceiling window flooded the room with light, and from the window, I could see a barn and the hill that lead to the retreat huts. I tried to like the room, to feel at home in it, but the nineteenth-century stone structure was drafty and cold, with no locks on any of the doors. Who needs locks, I asked myself, when you're living in a Sufi community? Home, however, is the place where you relax, where you feel secure enough to let down your guard. But I couldn't. I always felt a little tense, a little on edge.

What I hated most was sharing the community bathroom. I didn't know it then, but I was suffering through an onslaught of Crohn's disease, and at that point bathrooms were a frequent and vital part of my life. Having to use the communal facility added to the physical discomfort I was experiencing. *Never mind,* I told myself. *It's a commune. That's the point. You have to share things . . . like a bathroom. You'll get used to it.* But I never did.

As the sun set in the evenings, I would sit at my window and think of my daughters. My eldest daughter Renee was still living in Japan with her husband and now their son Akira. As I looked out at the Berkshire Mountains, I tried to imagine the mountains of Japan. Were the sunsets there as bright as the ones here? Were they as golden, as daunting red? My children felt very far away from the life I was living now.

We grew our own vegetables and fruits, and our meals were strictly vegetarian, except for occasional holidays or celebrations. Every lunch and dinner was a combo of tofu, rice, and vegetables in various disguises. Pasta showed up now and then, but not very many of the residents knew how to cook it, let alone make a good sauce. As an Italian, I felt as though I were in one of Dante's hellish realms. Tomato sauce is *not* meant to be something that comes out of a can! I could almost hear my grandmother's groans from the grave. When I sat down to a steaming plate of tofu lasagna, with not a shred of ricotta or mozzarella to be seen, I wished *I* were in my grave!

All of us had kitchen duty; we could choose between cooking and cleanup. Most of the residents preferred cooking. I've never much liked cooking, though I'm a competent cook, and cooking vegetables to the consistency of baby food was certainly not my heart's desire. I volunteered for cleanup. The grueling labor felt like some form of medieval penance, but occasionally, I'd get a respite.

"Bahri, are you ready?" Aftab would call. "We're going out to dinner!"

"You bet I'm ready!" I'd shout back. "What took you and Hope so long?"

These two women, Aftab and Hope, kept me sane. Aftab, whose name means "sun" in Arabic, was a bright, happy little blonde, while Hope was tall, with prematurely white hair and the husky voice of a femme fatale. When I asked her once why she had kept her baptismal name, she said, "Because I'm *hoping* my faith in God will grow. That's why I'm here. But so far, the outlook's not promising."

During this period of my life, I frequently found myself floating in some hazy gray place halfway between my longing for the spiritual heights and my hatred of the communal bathroom—but Aftab and Hope pulled me into focus. They grounded me. They were never awestruck by the spirituality of the place, nor did they believe in miracles. They loved a good martini, they liked to laugh, and they never hesitated to say an expletive as needed.

Once every two weeks, the three of us would leave the Abode . . . and go directly to the nearest steakhouse. We savored each medium-rare bite like inmates on death row.

"You'd think that with all the land the Abode owns," Hope said one night between bites, "we could raise a few cows and get steak now and then."

"We don't have the manpower or the knowhow," Aftab said with her mouth full, "and you *know* that."

"We don't have the incentive either." Hope made a face. "These kids, they think that eating vegetarian meals will allow their energy to *flow*. As though that will make them holier. As though it will make them see angels or something. Throw in some crystals, and they think they'll be floating off to another realm. You can *tell* that's what they think. You can read it all over their tender little faces!"

"Hope, stop it." But Aftab was giggling even as she protested. "They're young. Their spirituality hasn't matured yet."

"Neither have their brains."

"Will you stop it, Hope? You're going to worry Bahri." Aftab signaled to the waiter. "Come on, you two, have another drink. You'll feel better in no time."

I loved these two women, and I knew they loved me. We were all about the same age, we all had grown children, and we were all big-city girls. We understood each other. And yet we each had our own reasons for being at the Abode.

Aftab was there because she had fallen in love, both with Hazrat Inayat Khan and with Sufism. Like the great medieval Sufi poets, Aftab was both earthy and spiritual, overflowing with down-to-earth laughter and deep sanctity. Years later, after a long hospitalization, she went into a coma from which she was not expected to emerge—and then one day, her eyes popped open. She looked at the people around her bed and exclaimed, "I forgot to die!" Everyone burst into startled laughter. Aftab never stopped being Aftab.

Hope, on the other hand, was far less spiritual. She had come to the Abode mainly to be with Aftab, though she always hoped for a spiritual transformation that never came. Her views of the Abode were consistently cynical, if not downright negative—but she could always make Aftab and me laugh.

These two women—and the friendship they gave me—were truly the best part of my time at the Abode.

***

Every year around Labor Day, Pir Vilayat gave a yearly retreat. People came from all over the world. Since there was not enough room at the Abode, two huge tents were set up on top of a mountain. One tent accommodated the daily conferences, and the other was used to serve meals. Outhouses and outdoor showers were provided, but we slept in our own tents. I had bought myself a pup tent for the occasion.

"How in hell am I supposed to put this thing up?" I screamed at Aftab as I struggled with the bundle of poles and nylon.

"Shh, Bahri, I'll show you. There's nothing to it."

Hope gave a snort of laughter. "Right!" she said. "Nothing to it!"

Aftab ignored us both. With the sweet, calm voice of a kindergarten teacher instructing a five-year-old, she showed me step by step how to erect my shelter. "There!" She stepped back and beamed at me. "You see? You did it!"

"Want your cherry lollypop now?" Hope drawled.

"Shut up!" I told her, but I was laughing.

We were still laughing as we made our way to the conference tent. Beneath its wide expanse, we found Pir Vilayat dressed in his white robe, his white hair and beard flowing over his chest and shoulders. Although he wasn't tall, he seemed to me like a giant, glowing white in the tent's shadows. When he began speaking, his soft voice with its cultured British accent calmed our laughter. As he led the crowd in meditation, Aftab, Hope, and I settled down.

Pir Vilayat's meditations were a new experience for me. At Columbia University, I had known him as a lecturer, but here I experienced him differently. Propping himself up on a plank where we could all see him, he assumed a lotus position. He was using a microphone, but his voice was very soft. "Close your eyes," he told us. "Sit in stillness."

After we had sat silently for several moments, he led us into a guided mediation. No music, song, or movement accompanied him. The whisper of the wind in the trees was the only background to his voice as he led us first through the astral plane, the spiritual realm that is a kind of limbo where spirits dwell before they incarnate into a physical body. Using only the power of his voice, he then transported us to the jinn plane, another spiritual universe, but this one of intellect and mind. In the world of the jinns, however, the mind is only a design, a pattern of potential, for only the experience of life on Earth completes the making of the mind. We then came to the angelic plane where angels dwell. Angels, Pir told us, see with the clarity of the innocent. "The relations of angels to human beings is that of a little child to a grown-up person," he said. "They can help human beings as an infant can help its elders." Then, finally, he led us to the causal plane, the plane where archetypes of all created things are found in the form of pure vibrations, vibrations that first create sound . . . and then burst forth into light.

Worlds beyond worlds, all of them beyond the material world of pup tents and kitchen chores and everyday frustrations. These were new levels of consciousness, and the images Pir used pointed to a greater reality beyond our ability to comprehend. As I followed his voice, my understanding of creation expanded. I felt I was looking out at a great expanse, a sweep of reality so broad that it contained not only the Earth and its inhabitants but also huge swathes of other realms. Surrounded by this enormous perspective, I felt very small—and yet at the same time, I knew my tiny life mattered. I was not insignificant, for I was part of this immense magnificence. I was precious to the One who loved it all.

After the meditation, we remained sitting. No one wanted to move. Peace streamed through me like flowing water.

When I opened my eyes at last, Pir Vilayat looked as if he had been transported somewhere beyond our reach. Slowly, one by one, each of us rose and left the tent. I made my way to my little tent, but the peace remained with me for the duration of the retreat.

During that time, Pir led us in more meditations, and with each succeeding one, I perceived the world around me being transformed into a brighter and brighter light, until even the trees, the grass, and the stones seemed to glow. No doubt everyone who attended that retreat had a different experience. I am certain, though, that each of us felt the holiness in Pir's voice, in his words, and in the silence.

That Labor Day retreat was only the beginning. Since Pir's own spiritual understanding was continually evolving, every retreat he lead was new. The new depths didn't cancel the old or replace it but only built on it. Pir's level of consciousness made it hard for us to keep up with him.

"I don't know what he's saying half the time!" Hope complained. "I wish he'd speak English, for God's sake! I never even had a college education, while this guy went to Oxford. How does he expect someone like me to understand?"

Aftab tried to explain. "Look, Hope, you just take what you can—and let the rest go. You don't have to understand everything. God gives you whatever you need to nourish your soul. The rest is just extra. Let it pass through you and don't worry about it. Don't get nuts about it. Just enjoy it!"

"There you go again, Aftab," I said, "making it all sound so easy. I for one read spiritual books like crazy, and I understand them and enjoy them. But when it comes to Pir, I just don't get everything he says. I feel like I'm understanding it, but it doesn't stick somehow. I can't retain it."

"Thank you, Bahri," Hope said. "And *you* have a college education. No wonder I'm lost."

Aftab wrapped her arms around Hope. "But you understand with your heart, and that's all that matters."

"Damn it, Aftab, you're incorrigible!" Hope looked at me over Aftab's blonde head and winked. "So help me, after this retreat I'm treating myself to a martini, a steak, and a dirty movie!"

Aftab laughed. "Now who's being incorrigible!"

When the retreats were over, I constantly struggled to recall Pir's words. Even when I could, they no longer had the power to lead me into other realms as they had when I heard him speak. My experiences as I listened to Pir now felt like dreams, and the old doubts once more began to play with my head.

And yet another part of me was content to have simply been with Pir. Something real happened during those meditations, something that changed me. I didn't need to understand his words with my intellect; I didn't even need to remember them. Regardless of my brain's ability to keep up, my spirit was nourished.

✳✳✳

In between these intense spiritual experiences with Pir, my life fell into a pattern. On Monday evenings, we all attended classes to hear what the Masters had to say about Sufism and the Path in general. During the remainder of the week, I went to healing classes and prepared for ordination. I had begun studying for ordination back in my old life, but it wasn't until I lived at the Abode that I completed my studies and Pir Vilayat ordained me.

After the ceremony, he looked at me and called me "Reverend." I was startled, for somehow it had not occurred to me until then that I would now be a member of the clergy. Within the Order, or course, those of us who were ordained were not called reverends but rather

cherags (masculine) or *cheragas* (feminine). Nevertheless, we did all the things that many clergy do: presided
over the worship service, baptized children, blessed and
purified houses, and performed marriages.

Now that I was ordained, Aftab and I would often on
Sunday evenings bring the Universal Worship service to
people in Albany who were unable to attend the morning
service at the Abode. They weren't Sufis, simply people
who loved our worship service. If, for whatever reason,
they couldn't attend the morning Sunday service, we'd
bring it to them in the evening. Depending upon the
number of people attending, we'd hold the service in
someone's house or in an auditorium. We'd set up the
scriptures from the major religions on the altar, exactly
as we did during the service at the Abode, and then we
read what each scripture pronounced about the chosen
theme (anything from world peace to divorce). Before
reading the holy words, though, we chanted, danced, or
read poetry to honor each religion. The service always
ended with a Sufi dance. I loved the joy I felt giving this
service, especially to those who couldn't attend services
at the Abode due to age or illness. I sensed the service
was the best thing we could do for them—and at the
same time, it was the best thing I could do for myself
as well. The joy and gratitude exchanged there were a
wonderful way to start a new week.

During my time at the Abode, I also taught at a high
school in Massachusetts. This way I could still earn a
living, since salaried jobs at the Abode were limited to

working on the farm, in the elementary school, or in the main office. Aftab held the only job in the bookstore.

The students at Stockbridge High School were smarter, better dressed, more respectful, and more affluent than those I had taught on Long Island. Both the students' parents and the administrators treated the teachers like royalty. For the first time in my teaching career, I was granted a desk and private space outside the classroom. Every once in a while, fresh flowers appeared on my desk.

But despite all that, I didn't enjoy teaching. The administration and teachers had no idea I was living at the Abode, and I felt a little like an imposter. The school's staff were good, conventional people who worked hard, focused on the school and students, but the constant conversations about discipline, grades, and curriculum bored me. I wondered if they would throw me out if they realized the alternative lifestyle I was living.

When I was teaching, I yearned to be back at the Abode—but at the same time, life at the Abode was both slower and harder than I had imagined. I wanted more spiritual and intellectual stimulation than I was getting. Sufi classes and Universal Worship amounted to a few hours a week, not enough to satisfy my hunger for *more*.

At the same time, screening for entrance into the Abode had become less strict. The receiving committee was allowing people into the Abode who had no real interest in Sufi spirituality. Many of them were vagrants, people who were simply looking for a rent-free place to live. With so many people there who did not share our spiritual goals, the atmosphere became diluted somehow, as though the rigor and intensity of Pir's teaching was being watered down. At last, as the leaders realized how detrimental this atmosphere was for the rest of us, the drifters were asked to leave.

Meanwhile, I was ready to have my own place. I decided to have an apartment built in one of the main buildings. Partly, I wanted a place where my daughters could be more comfortable when they visited me. Nicole, my youngest daughter, visited me often during her college breaks. She loved the Abode, which suited her temperament; she worked in the gardens while she was there and made friends easily. I saw a budding spirituality in her that today continues to grow and flourish. Renee also visited with her Japanese husband, and they both enjoyed being at the Abode. In many respects, they told me, its gentle and calm atmosphere was a little like Japan. They felt at home with the soft-spoken people who treated one another with the utmost respect. Denise, however, my little Jewish convert, never visited me, despite the many Sufis of Jewish faith who resided there. I don't think it was her Jewishness that kept her away, though; I suspect she was embarrassed by her forty-five-year-old mother living in a commune like an aging hippie. Besides, Denise's strengths and talents were active and vital, more suited to the challenge of life outside the Abode rather than the gentle quiet within it. And so I contented myself with visits from my other two daughters.

After three months of construction, the apartment was finally ready for me to move into it. Extending from one end of the building to the other, a huge room without walls contained the living, cooking, and dining areas; beyond the only dividing wall were a bath and a bedroom with a loft. The windows in the apartment faced the Berkshires, blessing me with views of sunsets and mountains.

I was dependent on a small woodstove for heat. A gentleman at the Abode tried earnestly, even desperately, to teach me how to split logs but to no avail. I wasn't strong enough to manage the feat of chopping wood into stove-size chunks, nor did I particularly want to. Instead, I paid to have them cut and stacked in a convenient spot in the apartment.

One winter night, I woke shivering in the middle of the night, the air against my face like ice. I wrapped a blanket around my pajamas and ran to the stove. Just as I feared, the fire had gone out. I shoved a few logs into the stove and tried to light them—but they just sat there, cold and black, while again and again the small flicker of the matches went dark. My hands were shaking, and I was nearly crying with frustration, but each time I lit another match, the logs stubbornly refused to catch. I pulled the blanket tighter around me and looked outside the window at the thermometer: 30 degrees below zero. I was sure Aftab and Hope would discover my frozen body in the morning.

I survived of course. The next day, I practiced building fires until I was finally proficient at lighting the stove.

The threat of cold hung over me, though, and I came to hate winter.

During those short, dark days and long, cold nights, I found myself remembering again the winters of my adolescence, those dreary days when I'd played hooky from school, overwhelmed with guilt and desperation. I remembered too the winters of my daughters' baby-hoods, the days when I had felt trapped in the house while my husband went off to work every day. For me, winter had become a symbol of loneliness. It brought to life in me the old sense of abandonment I'd experienced as a child.

As a child I had feared I might die if my mother were to reject me, and now I sensed that death lurked in the cold and dark. Was it my own death I feared? Or God's? The snow and wind whispered that God had abandoned me all over again. I feared the Divine would never return to me—and at the same time, I feared what God would do to me if He did come back. I felt guilty and lonely and scared.

We form our primitive concepts of God in our parents' images, and these deep primal ideas are hard to remove from our unconscious. During the remainder of my time at the Abode, each time the fire in the stove went out, these bleak feelings rose in me anew. With the return of warmth, I tried to forget the terror and loneliness of the cold. But they never went away altogether. Even today, when I understand that cold, darkness, and even death are only manifestations of the Divine mystery, whenever winter falls, I still battle the old cold fear. Am I really loved? And if not, how can I exist?

I had good friends at the Abode, and I had experienced deep spiritual satisfaction there. I had my own place there now, with my very own bathroom. But as my forgotten fears stirred to life, a new restlessness filled me. For a long time, I had managed to hide my initial response to the Abode from my own awareness, the sense that I didn't belong here. It had lain sleeping, buried so deeply I had forgotten it existed, but now it woke up. I still didn't want to face this feeling. I didn't want it to be true.

But I couldn't make it go back to sleep.

12

Truly, it is in darkness
that one finds the light.

Meister Eckhart

One day while I was in the Abode office, I picked up a brochure that described a two-year course in spiritual guidance, sponsored by an organization called the Guild for Spiritual Formation. I glanced at the brochure, then began to read it more carefully. The course was designed, it said, to train spiritual guides through the study of Carl Jung, Teilhard de Chardin, and the Christian mystics.

Something inside me—my heart?—flip-flopped down to my solar plexus and back again. I was instantly convinced that I had to apply to this program. Quickly, I filled out the necessary forms, wrote the prerequisite essay, and sent them in. Within weeks I was accepted.

The Quaker author John Yungblut had founded the Guild, and he was one of our teachers. With him on the faculty were Sister Cora from Marymount College, an Episcopal parish priest, and a laywoman who was a

Teilhardian scholar. The two-year course was given on weekends in the Wainwright House in Rye, New York.

I loved the mansion with its atmosphere of gracious living from a bygone age. Meals were served with fine china and crystal goblets; during the day, we read and studied in two sunrooms, a living room, and a library, while at night we slept in the bedrooms on the second and third floors. We walked on a stone path along the edge of Long Island Sound.

In my memory, the Abode is often covered in with snow and cold, but when I think of my time in the Guild for Spiritual Formation, I remember the bright colors of tulips and forsythia, the scent of lilacs. Even in winter, the walk was lined with the fiery red berries of holly bushes, bright against the snow. After the Abode's quiet monotone, I felt surrounded by extravagant color. And instead of the colorless, tasteless tofu dishes served at the Abode, the weekend began with the rich flavors of wine and cheese before dinner.

After dinner, Sister Cora would teach a session on the Christian mystics. She had a gift for making each mystic come alive for us, and for the first time, I was beginning to understand these strange souls the Church had often considered to be too "esoteric" or even dangerous. The next day, we concentrated on Jung and Teilhard, two men of genius who approached reality from opposite directions: Jung from the perspective of the inner function of the human being, and Teilhard from the outer working of the cosmos. Sunday mornings were devoted to a recap, discussion, and role-playing the relationship between a spiritual guide and a follower. Finally, on Sunday afternoons, we engaged in what we laughingly referred to as group therapy.

I loved almost all of it. My hungry mind and spirit were finally being fed. But I hated Sunday afternoons. John Yungblut and I had become good friends, so I wasn't hesitant when I brought up the group therapy sessions to him.

"John, why do we need them? We discuss everything as a group anyway. They're a waste of time!"

John just grinned. "You know why, Bahri. Otherwise, you wouldn't resist them so much. Remember what Jung said. We must see into our own Shadows, the dark and hidden parts of our unconscious. That's the only way to truly understand ourselves—and God. I admit our group sessions don't go deep enough. But they provide a framework for more in-depth study of ourselves in the future."

I shook my head in exasperation. "No, John, that's not why I hate these sessions. These people don't want to go into their Shadows—and you know it! They're terrified of what they might find in their own darkness. So instead, they keep passing the buck. And what drives me straight up the wall—they do it with such sanctimony, all smiles and sweetness. I sit there wishing I could haul off and—"
I threw up my hands. "Facing our shadows be damned! They're all way too proper for that!"

John smiled at me, but for a long moment he said nothing. "Bahri," he said at last, "will you do something for me?"

"What?" I looked at him suspiciously, wondering if I'd gone too far after all.

"Become our bullshit detector."

"Become your *what?*"

"You know what I mean. Call them on their phoniness and their sanctimony. Don't let them get away with it! Speak out. Let your voice be heard. If you can do this, it would be a great service to the group."

"Aw, c'mon John." I narrowed my eyes and glared at him. "Don't do this to me. I won't have a friend left!"

He laughed. "Well, think about it. Promise?"

"Okay." I sighed. "*Bullshit detector . . .* oh God!"

But I tried. *Let your voice be heard,* John had told me, and those words called to me. No one had ever spoken them to me before. I couldn't resist answering their call.

Some in the group appreciated my efforts; others didn't. As I used my voice to be a "bullshit detector," something else happened that I hadn't expected: I couldn't point out others' phoniness without confronting my own. I had to take a long, hard look at my own particular brand of pretension and false holiness. My own shadow had dark depths I had never yet dared to probe.

Let your voice be heard. The words lingered in my head. John had affirmed a part of me I was still trying to identify, still trying to bring out into the open: the part of me that had something to say to say to the world. With all my responsibilities at the Abode, I still didn't have the sense that I was using my own voice.

John must have known what he was doing. But it was still hard to believe that I truly had the authority to speak. Why would anyone want to listen to *me?*

***

Despite the discomfort and challenge of looking into my own shadowlands, I was happy at Wainwright House. When I left at the end of every weekend and went back to the Abode, however, a sense of melancholy always went with me. I loved the intellectual challenge I experienced in the Guild, I loved learning, and I loved the sense of dignity and respect that illuminated the teachings and made them concrete. Each Sunday night, I left with a sad heart.

The words of the Sufi master Abu Sa'id Abul-Khayr brought me comfort:

> *The tear that falls from my separation from You*
> *I turn into a pearl,*
> *and with the thread of life, I make a rosary of it.*
> *Then, with these beads in hand,*
> *I seat myself in the heart's cell of solitude,*
> *and repeat Your name.*

Loss, emptiness, loneliness, abandonment—the very things I feared most—and yet somehow, even these could lead me to the One who loved me. *I seat myself in the heart's cell of solitude and repeat Your name:* was *this* the song I needed to sing? And could I do it, even in utter solitude, even in loneliness?

I still did not have the answers to these questions, but slowly, the questions themselves made me realize that life at the Abode was not the right one for me. The phrase "I'm out of my element" kept recurring in my mind, as though I were a bird trying to live underwater or a fish doing its best to breathe air. The Abode was not my natural element. I was not equipped to breathe in its atmosphere—and without the psychic oxygen I needed, how could I hope to speak, to sing?

I had told myself I had come to the Abode to serve God. And yes, I presided over Universal Worship, gave classes, led retreats. But as I screwed up my nerve to peer into my Shadow, I wondered if all I was doing was not my own version of phony sanctimoniousness, a way to fool myself while I continued to silence my own rejected voice.

The fear that struck my heart on cold winter nights . . . the sadness I felt whenever I returned to the Abode . . . the sense I'd had ever since I came to the Abode of being dislocated, as though my heart and my surroundings were painfully out of joint . . . all these whispered to me: *You have failed. You have failed yourself.*

But, I protested, *I came to the Abode to work for God. I came to find security. I came to put myself at the very heart of Sufism, where my future will be safe and secure.*

The small, long-buried voice within me was not convinced. *Bullshit,* she whispered. *Bullshit.*

I couldn't bear to listen. The message was unbearable. Had I really given up everything—my home, my professional life, my financial security—for a silly whim? I didn't dare to think that.

I hated the voice that whispered these fears in my heart. Its soft, insistent words terrified me. And so I once again muffled that voice. I refused to look any longer into the place from which it spoke. Instead, I turned outward, hoping for something new to come along, a new spiritual adventure, something that would save me, change me, without me ever having to look inside my own darkness.

The days went by, and I endured each one, hiding my unhappiness even from myself, hoping for some magical metamorphosis that would come to me from the world around me. Another winter ended.

Then, when spring came, two Sufi leaders offered everyone at the Abode a trip to Greece and the Holy Land. I knew beyond doubt that I had to go.

13

When you leave me in the grave,
don't say good-bye.
Remember, a grave is only paradise's curtain.
You saw me buried. Now watch me rise.
How can there be an end to life?
When the sun sets or the moon goes down,
it looks like the end,
but in another land, that sunset is the dawn.
When you let yourself be locked in the grave,
your soul will rise up free.

Rumi

I quit my teaching job, much to the astonishment of the administration and faculty, and off I went with fifteen others to visit the Holy Land. My excitement—or was it anxiety?—was so great I became ill on the plane. By the time we reached Greece, I was sick enough that I had to go to bed. I never had a chance to enjoy that ancient and beautiful land.

Israel, however, was another story. I never quite believed people who said, "I felt like I was coming home," when they talked about going to some foreign country. I disliked the cliché—and yet these were the very words that struck me as I stepped off the plane onto Jerusalem's soil. The sense of homecoming that washed over me was so powerful that I wanted to drop to my knees and kiss the ground.

Once Aftab and I checked into our hotel room, we took a walk around the Old City. I had expected to see something that looked like a movie set for some biblical film; instead, as we walked along the Via Dolorosa, we passed stores and street vendors. We ducked under clotheslines and dodged people who all seemed to be arguing with each other. The smell of money was everywhere. *This* was the route Jesus took on his way to Calvary?

Later, when I mentioned my sense of shock to our group leader, he shook his head. "All this is good." He waved his hand at the noise and gaudy signs. "It shows humanity. It is as it should be."

So much for my romantic notions about the Holy Land. Apparently, God loves screaming street vendors, dirty streets, and endless goods for sale as much as quiet hills and the gentle lap of waves.

No one simply *buys* anything in Jerusalem, I soon discovered. It's nothing so simple as checking a price tag and handing over your money. Instead, you bargain—sometimes for hours—haggling in different languages, until one of you—either you or the vendor—gets so tired you no longer care. Then you throw up your hands, throw down your money, and walk away with your new possession. I found I enjoyed it, maybe because my own insistent voice had a chance to speak. The vendor wasn't going to be hurt if I was less than sweet, if I was fierce enough to raise my voice. Locked in our battle of words, we each respected the other's stubbornness. It was lots of fun.

On the day we visited Calvary, I was expecting to see crosses on a bare hill. No such hill existed. Instead, we made our way between crowded attached houses, while barefoot children held out their hands along the streets, begging for pennies, and the adults watched our every move with narrow eyes. Tourists were there as well, navigating in and out of alleyways, restaurants, and shops. In the distance, within the Old City, the Church of the Holy Sepulcher lifted its blue domes into the bluer sky. The church would be our next stop.

Archeologists debate where Jesus was buried. Some say outside of the Old City, but according to Orthodox tradition, he was buried in a tomb that now lies somewhere beneath the lower level of the Church of the Holy Sepulcher. As I stepped into the church's shadowy cavern, I looked up at hundreds of lit candles in gold and silver votive holders hanging from the ceiling. They cast their flickering light over the church's gold, gold that was everywhere. Gold-encased icons, altars that glimmered with gold leaf, stained-glass windows with golden borders. The candles and the gleam of gold, however, were not enough to light the church. Even after my eyes adjusted from the outside light, the church's great nave was a dark hollow into which I entered slowly, step by step.

Along with the rest of my group as well as a few other tourists, I passed through the Chapel of Angels that served as an anteroom to the actual tomb. The chapel glittered with more ornate gold; a small, carved marble doorway led down into the tomb. The Orthodox monk who guarded the tomb cautioned us to lower our heads as we entered the small space that only accommodated six or seven people. On top of what looked like a stone coffin was a glass box filled with coins. The presence of money even here in this small and holy space seemed jarring.

Look deeper, whispered a voice inside me. I could be affronted and pious, allowing my culture shock to stand between me and the strange and lovely reality of this dusty land—or I could choose to look past all that offended my sensibilities.

Then, as I gazed at those gold coins resting over the spot where once the dead body of Jesus Christ may have rested, suddenly, past, present, and future merged into a single moment. Hope and history, greed and love, miracle and money, all slammed together in a cataclysmic union. I was no longer aware of the others around me. I knew only that there was nowhere in the entire world to go, nowhere to be, but here; there was nothing I needed to do or work for but *this*.

And then I had to leave, to make room for the next group. I didn't want to go; it seemed almost physically painful to place one foot in front of the other and leave this small space. As I went through the doorway, back into the Chapel of Angels, I forgot to duck my head, and my skull banged against the stone. The pain was sickening, and yet at the same time I welcomed it as yet another strange and unexpected gift. In an unknown and unknowable way, the pain allowed me to carry in my own flesh a reminder of Christ's continual suffering. Even today, when I recall that moment and the pain in my head, I feel a sense of gladness.

But that night in my hotel room, while Aftab slept in the bed beside me, I couldn't stop thinking about Jesus Christ, this man who might have been buried in that tomb I had visited, who might have risen again from the dead. Who was he to me? Anything at all? Did his life and death matter to me?

Back in the days when I had considered myself a Christian, Jesus had never seemed all that important. He was just a bloody guy hanging on a cross. In pictures of the crucifixion, he was always surrounded by a crowd of women looking up at him, their faces anguished, while he gazed down at them with a long-suffering expression. With all those women adoring him, he didn't need me. He had them.

The Church told me I should feel guilt for his death, as though I were somehow personally responsible for the pain he was suffering on that cross. I resented the guilt being thrust on me; I'd had enough of people who used guilt to manipulate me. In fact, I didn't much like Jesus at all. Mary was the one I had loved as a child, and Mary was the one who had brought me a new sense of Divine love during the Sufi retreats. Jesus was only a masculine presence bleeding in the background. I was tired of his sorrowful expression.

And yet in one of my experiences with Mary, I had felt she was showing me her Son, the Light that was greater than she. When I came to live at the Abode, I was surprised to discover that so many Christians lived there, and I also became convinced that the Sufi sheiks loved Jesus far more than I ever had. I began to feel that this guy, this Son of God, was haunting me in some strange way I didn't understand.

That term—Son of God—annoyed me. What did it mean? When the founder of my Sufi order was asked about Christ's relationship to God, he replied, "If we can't find God in a human being, where else are we going to find him?" I liked the answer, and yet it didn't quite satisfy me. I had been well indoctrinated as a Catholic child on Christ's specific and unique role; how could I make sense of that in light of my beliefs as a Sufi? Did I need to?

Jesus continued to haunt me. His presence there in the background of my spiritual experiences pulled at me, as though he were gently but insistently dragging my attention toward him. It was a subtle haunting; he was not a noisy or demanding ghost, but he never went away. I didn't like it. I didn't want to be pulled. I wanted my spiritual path to remain clear and open, free from all the old indoctrination I had put behind me.

But Jesus was persistent. I felt as though I had shut him in his grave again and again throughout my life—but like the Phoenix, he kept springing into fiery and indomitable life. And now that I had stood in the same place where many believed his flesh-and-blood body had actually lain, now that I had experienced that strange sense of powerful and living unity, how could I continue to ignore him?

I fell asleep at last, the question still unanswered.

✳✳✳

The next day, when we visited the Jewish section of the Old City, we went directly to its most famous site, the Wailing Wall. Legend has it that these stones are what's left of Solomon's wall; legend also says that if you write your prayer on a slip of paper and tuck it in a crevice between the stones, your prayer will be granted. At first I wasn't inclined to do this, but then I changed my mind. When my hand touched the wall to place my prayer between its stones, a deluge of images swept over me: the torture of the Jewish people down through the years, the unbearable suffering, the Holocaust . . . My own pain seemed so small by comparison. I looked at all those tiny scraps of paper fluttering between the stones, and I knew that each prayer was an expression of faith, a faith that had endured as long as stone, despite the centuries of persecution. I wept.

We went next to the Muslim section of the Old City. Since our arrival in Jerusalem, I had seen the sunshine glittering on the startling gold curves of the Dome of the Rock, and it had drawn me to it even as it frightened me a little. I might be a Sufi, but I didn't identify with Muslims; I had plenty of prejudices still intact. Today, we would visit the dome at last, and I worried that we wouldn't be allowed to enter. I also feared that as a woman, I'd be looked down upon.

I was wrong: we were welcomed. I covered my head with a scarf, stepped out of my shoes, and gazed around me at the intricate blue, white, and gold mosaics that covered the walls. Stone columns supported the ceiling's golden circle, and the entire space was bathed with light. Unlike the ornate Church of the Holy Sepulcher, I felt that this space was far simpler. It was a container for light.

At the front of the mosque, men were continually prostrating themselves as they uttered prayers in Arabic. I couldn't see their faces from my place at the back of the mosque, but from the way their bodies moved and the timber of their voices, I sensed that their prayers were no rote observance done out of a sense of duty. Their profound adoration of Allah filled the entire mosque.

✳✳✳

On another afternoon, I decided to go for a walk alone. As I walked down a narrow street, I came upon an old man sitting in front of an apartment building. I eyed him a little nervously, and when he held his hand out as if to stop me, I was about to make a run for it. Before I could edge past him, he blurted, "Are you Christian?"

Startled, I nodded my head.

His gaze seemed to hold both love and pain. "It is all the same. Allah is Allah. Different names, but same Allah. It is the same. Allah is Allah." His eyes filled with tears.

I placed my hand on his arm, needing to touch him, to physically express my sense that he and I were intimately joined. "Yes," I whispered.

I hesitated there on the street, expecting him to say more, but he looked away. After a moment, I continued my walk.

I never forgot his face, though, or the expression in his dark eyes.

✳✳✳

Jerusalem, with its three faiths swirling through its streets, was for me a sort of crucible. Within its walls, I was confronted with the Divine everywhere I turned, but always in different forms. The Church of the Holy Sepulcher, the Wailing Wall, the Dome of the Rock, all had offered me powerful, spiritual experiences. I had been searching for so long for *the answer*, the definitive way forward that would lead me to peace and fulfillment, but instead, each experience seemed only to point toward a deeper mystery.

One morning, we rose before dawn and went to see Ethiopian monks who lived on a rooftop. They were clothed in rags, yet their bronze skin, high foreheads, and sharp cheekbones made them look like gods. These men were contemplatives who prayed day and night for the good of the world. Their prayer began before dawn and ended far into the night. We weren't told how they survived. No one seemed to know where they got their food; perhaps they were beggars.

As I stood watching them, listening to their prayers, I was once more confronted with a sense of deep and sacred mystery. I read the monks' surrender to God in their very bodies, and each word they uttered vibrated with their humility and love. I knew I had been blessed with yet another unforgettable memory.

✳✳✳

The final stop of our tour of the Holy Land was at the Sea of Galilee. After the noise and busyness of Jerusalem, its unearthly beauty took me by surprise. When I reach heaven, I expect it to look like this spot.

We went to the Franciscan monastery that was built so close to the shore that the sea nearly lapped at its walls. The monastery's white walls and round red roofs rose from the silence like flower buds. Here was another deeply holy place. The Divine seemed nearly tangible in this quiet place.

After we had finished our tour, we were all hushed, nearly surfeited with holiness. We decided to have dinner together at a restaurant we had spotted along the road. The sign above the building announced that the place was called "Peter's Fish," and since our trip was quickly coming to an end, we were hoping to extend our time together by sharing a meal instead of going back to the hotel.

But when we told our plan to the bus driver, he looked horrified. "Are you people nuts? Don't you know that nobody stays out after dark? You can have your dinner if you want, but don't expect me to wait around for you. I'm leaving! I'm not risking being shot, not me!"

So much for the lovely sense of peace we'd been feeling! And so much for "Peter's Fish." We went back to the hotel.

✳✳✳

The next day, most of our group went home. The only exceptions were a priest, an older woman—and me. We decided to visit Egypt.

It was my Sufi name that lured me there. I had learned that "Bahri" was also the name of the place where Queen Hatshepsut had built herself a temple.

Hatshepsut, who ruled during Egypt's Eighteenth Dynasty, is sometimes portrayed wearing a beard, symbolic of her power as pharaoh, while in other statues she is identified with Sekhmet, the lion-headed goddess of both war and healing. Hatshepsut was a wise ruler, and Egypt prospered under her reign, economically, socially, and militarily. She built many temples, including the one dedicated to herself at Deir el-Bahri in the desert near Luxor.

I wanted to see this temple. Perhaps I thought I would gain some new insight there that would lead me further along my inner journey. I may have hoped that this long-ago woman's strong spirit would somehow rub off on me. Or perhaps, spiritual junky that I was, I was simply seeking yet one more mystical adventure.

Deir el-Bahri was a surprisingly modern-looking cluster of buildings with long clean lines, built from the same sand-colored stone as the cliff that rose sharply behind them. The focal point of the complex was the Djeser-Djeseru, the Holy of Holies: the Mortuary Temple of Hatshepsut, which sat atop a series of terraces reached by long ramps.

As we explored the ancient structure, our guide told us more about Hatshepsut. She had lived nearly fifteen hundred years before Christ, he told us, but she was still considered to be one of the greatest and wisest of Egypt's rulers. "She is also known as *Ma'at-ka-re*," he said, "which means 'spirit of harmony and truth.'" He then went on to hint that Hatshepsut was currently busy helping the Virgin Mary bring peace to the Earth.

I was startled by the mention of Mary. Could there really be any connection between the woman I had loved all my life and this long-ago queen? And what of Christ? For so long, I had felt as though he were haunting me; in the Holy Land, he had been the ghost who dogged my footsteps as I walked the earth where he too had walked so many centuries before. Here in

Egypt, however, Christianity felt very young, as though by comparison, Jesus had been born only yesterday— and yet as I gazed at the relief sculptures depicting stories from Hatshepsut's life, I felt goose bumps rise along my arms. For a moment, the river of time that flowed between far distant points in history seemed to mean nothing at all.

That night we stayed at an old but elegant hotel. My high-ceilinged room was decorated with artifacts, and I slept enclosed within a flowing canopy of white gauze. As I climbed into the big bed, I felt a sense of foreboding, but I pushed it away with the thought that my friends were just down the hall.

My dreams while I was in Egypt were so strange that I still remember them. That night and each night that followed, I dreamed that an unseen, unidentified force pushed me down dark passageways and into deep caverns, thrusting me always deeper toward an unknown destination I never reached. In the morning, I awoke shaken and uneasy. I told myself that my own unconscious was simply reflecting the collective unconscious of an ancient land: the old, old culture buried now in the Earth's womb. Years later, however, I wonder if it weren't my own spiritual journey I was sensing in my dreams, the journey ever deeper into what Jung called the Shadow, even as I constantly sought a vision of Divine light.

Finally, we returned to Cairo. Since we still had a day until our flight home, we decided to use the time to tour

the Great Pyramid of Giza. We set off and found ourselves a guide.

"Call me Champion," he told us. "That is the meaning
of my name in English."

When we mentioned we were Sufis from America,
he gave us a wide, toothless smile. "I will take you then
where no tourists are allowed."

The three of us exchanged glances. "Is it okay, do you
think?" muttered the other woman in our little group.

The priest shrugged. "He's a certified tour guide. And
I for one am ready for an adventure."

So was I.

We followed Champion into the greatest pyramid
ever built. At first, he gave us the practiced spiel I was
sure he gave to all tourists.

"The Great Pyramid was built by Khufu, who is sometimes known as Cheops. He enslaved his people to build
this mighty edifice. It is built from more than two million
stone blocks, and each stone weighs between two and
fifteen tons. The pyramid was built so quickly—his slaves
must have had to set a block in place every two and a half
minutes. Imagine the labor!"

He led us through the chambers and galleries, and
then at last we followed him back into the daylight. "You
are ready now?" he asked us with a grin. "Now I shall take
you where no tourists go?"

We nodded our agreement, and he rummaged in his
bag, then pulled out four candles, one for each of us. "We
will need these," he told us and lit the wicks with a match.

We followed him back into the pyramid. This time, we went down a long hallway until we reached a spot where Champion dropped to his knees. He slid aside a stone panel, then looked up at us and beckoned. "Come. Follow me."

We crawled after him on our knees, holding our candles in front of us. Inside the narrow passageway, the flickering candlelight seemed only to emphasize the deep darkness we were entering. We crept along for an eternity, none of us speaking. My knees were sore, and the hand that held the candle was starting to shake from weariness and excitement. I could feel the weight of stone and darkness and long centuries pressing on me, and I was reminded of my dream—and yet I did not feel afraid, only curious.

At last, the darkness ahead of us grew lighter. Champion led us out of the tunnel and into a high room that seemed alight with sunshine, though I could see no windows. The room was empty except for a small stone sarcophagus.

Grateful to stand erect again, we stretched our cramped legs and gazed around us. The room was filled with fresh air and that mysterious light. "Where does it come from?" I asked Champion. "The light and the air?"

He gave me no answer, but instead, he clapped his hands with delight. "This room is for initiation. Man must prove that he worthy to become servant of the gods. So he stay in this"—he pointed to the sarcophagus—"for days, till king let him out. If still alive, he worthy. If not, he go home to Valley of Kings." Champion laughed, as though he had told a joke.

But we did not share his sense of humor, and suddenly, my skin itched with the need to escape this ancient place. I sensed that my two companions were as uneasy as I was.

Champion looked into our faces and laughed again. "You have enough? Good. We go now—but you remember this place."

We followed him back through the pyramid and out into the hot afternoon. Champion smiled at our sweaty, tired faces. "You did well, Sufis from America. Now come to my house, and I give you dinner!"

His house proved to be a large cave with a front courtyard. On the floor of the courtyard, his wife sat cooking chicken over a Bunsen burner. She did not speak English.

Champion motioned us into his home, where his daughter served us tea and then quickly left. Then his wife brought us food, and we ate hungrily, talking together of many things. By the end of the meal, the little Egyptian had become our friend.

"I am Christian," he said as he swallowed his last bite of chicken. "But I know Sufis. They love God. Because you say you are Sufi, I trust you. I show you what I never show other tourists."

That night, my last in Egypt, I lay in my bed in the hotel and thought back over the day. In the years since then, I have continued to muse on my detour to Egypt, recalling both my dreams and the hidden room where Champion took us. I feel as though Egypt still has something to tell me. The breadcrumb trail of my Sufi name's similarity to that of Queen Hatshepsut's temple had lured me here—but there had been something deeper waiting for me.

That night in the hotel, I was trying to understand what it was, but it was too soon for me to grasp it. I would need many more years before I could begin to decipher the meaning of that stone coffin buried deep in the pyramid's darkness and yet surrounded by light. All the while, the meaning was closer to me than my skin, but hidden within the dark caverns of my unconscious, just as I had experienced in the dreams.

And even then, so many years ago, I somehow sensed that the price to pay for its release was to lie in the coffin within the buried room and die. Die to who I thought I was, die to the beliefs that had molded a self I never was. Long ago, I had entombed my voice, my true self. I needed to break open the sarcophagus, so that my true self could be resurrected—but that could not happen until I was willing to put the false self in the tomb first. Without death, there is never new life.

As I flew back home the next day, I knew this journey would linger in my mind and heart forever. In the Holy Land, I had been confronted with new images of the

Divine, and in Egypt's ancient land, I had glimpsed the meaning of the resurrection in a new way.

But now it was time to go back to the Abode. As I dozed on the plane, letting my thoughts run both backward and forward, I realized how reluctant I was to pick up my old life. I reminded myself of how lovely the Abode was—and yet going back there seemed like crawling into a narrow container that had grown far too tight for me.

The Abode had become, I realized, yet another coffin.

14

If you want to be sure of the road under your feet,
you must close your eyes and walk in the dark. . . .
Like a blind person, you must lean on dark faith,
accept it as your guide and light,
and depend on nothing of what you understand,
taste, feel, or imagine.
Saint John of the Cross

Returning to the Abode wasn't easy. My sense of disloca-
tion resurfaced, and this time it wasn't as easily repressed.
I had convinced myself that my move to the Abode was
the answer to all my questions, the ultimate springboard
into a new life of service to God.

How easily we fool ourselves. How easily we're convinced of the rightness of our own actions, only to find
our certainty contaminated by doubt and confusion. I
had sold my house, given up my old job, said good-bye
to family and friends . . . and now, a gnawing sense of
disappointment clung to me, like a shy child clinging to
her mother's skirts.

As this metaphor for my feelings occurred to me, I found myself imagining an actual fearful child. She looked like me, I realized, the way I had looked when I was small. I was Bahri now—and yet here was this silent little Marietta, haunting me. I was dismayed to see her face.

The Abode had given me many happy moments, I reminded myself—ordination, retreats, giving and taking classes, even acting in small dramas on important occasions—and I had close friends here who were loyal and loving. Surely, I was not the same person I had been before. I was Bahri, not Marietta. After all I had experienced, all I had learned, I must have achieved *something.*

And yet one night, I found myself standing outside alone, filled with a terrible despair. "What is it You want from me?" I screamed up at the star-filled sky. "Why do You let me feel so scared? So confused? What good does it do me? What good does it do *You?* Why do you hide Yourself when I need You most? Why?" I was shaking with rage as I screamed the word again, "Why?"

The night was silent around me except for the whisper of the wind in the trees. The stars gave me no answer.

From my vantage point years later, I can look back on that moment and see that my longing for God was God's longing for me. My desperate question was also my answer, for I would not have desired God with such heartsickness if God had not already desired me. No one has expressed this better than the ninth-century Sufi, Abu Yazid Bayazid Bistami:

I focused myself on remembering God, knowing Him, loving Him, seeking Him. And when I was done, I saw that He had remembered me before I had remembered Him; that His knowledge of me had preceded my knowledge of Him, His love toward me had existed before my love of Him, and He had sought me before I had sought Him.

But I was blind. I clung to my expectation of what a Divine answer should be, while at the same time I clutched my sense of entitlement. I was grasping at emptiness, of course, and expectation and entitlement only hid from me the very thing I wanted most.

Discernment is always difficult. I began to suspect it had been only my ego—the false self I had created over the years—that had convinced me the Abode would give me a foothold on my long journey toward spiritual meaning. The only real accomplishment I saw now was the leadership position I had attained here. Had that prestige been what I had been actually seeking? Was I still somehow trying to achieve the exterior success my parents had craved for me?

At this point in my thinking, my thoughts would suddenly flip-flop. Perhaps, after all, it had been God's will that I come here, not for the small personal success I had achieved, but so that I could experience disappointment, unhappiness, and heartache for the good of my soul.

To this day, I'm not certain whether God led me to the Abode—or whether I went there for all the wrong reasons. I don't think it matters. According to an old proverb, "God writes straight with crooked lines," and in the words of the Apostle Paul, "all things work together for good." The Divine Creator works with whatever material is at hand. Regardless of my reasons for going there, my time at the Abode was exactly what I needed.

But I couldn't see that yet. In the weeks after I returned from Egypt and the Holy Land, I plunged into emotional and spiritual darkness. Looking back, I can see that I was in midst of what Saint John of the Cross called the "dark night of the soul."

The sixteenth-century Spanish mystic wrote love poetry to God that was as passionate as any Sufi's. "Oh night, my guide!" he wrote. "Oh night more friendly than the dawn! Oh tender night that tied lover and the loved one, loved one in the lover fused as one." In his book *The Dark Night of the Soul*, John explained in more depth his understanding of spiritual darkness:

> *If the understanding is to be united with Divine light, it must be purged of its natural light, brought into darkness. This darkness must continue for as long as is necessary to annihilate the soul's old habits of understanding. . . . The darkness is profound, horrible, and painful. It feels very real. . . . For this night is gradually drawing the spirit away from its ordinary experience of life so that it can be filled with the Divine fire, which first makes the soul black and dark, so that it seems worse than before, before it unites and transforms*

the soul into itself, just as fire transforms a log of wood into fire.

Years later, I can better grasp what John was saying. Our souls' "old habits of understanding" are created by society and culture, by education and family, by many voices coming at us from outside our deepest, truest selves. The soul's dark nights strip these habits from us, leaving us naked and afraid, with nothing familiar to hold on to. The external things that once made us happy—money, prestige, material success, the comfort of others' voices telling us who we are—no longer satisfy us. In desperation, we are driven deeper into the darkness, into ourselves.

I had thought myself so wise. During all those years of intense spiritual exploration, I had been piling up mystical experiences, accumulating spiritual achievements— and now I simply felt silly and deluded. I tried to think rationally and maturely about my situation. *Knock it off!* I'd tell myself. *You're a grown woman who is having a bit of a bad time, that's all. Stop making such a big deal out of it. Stop feeling so sorry for yourself!*

But I did feel sorry for myself. I felt God had abandoned me, taking away from me any sense of spiritual comfort, so that I was right back to being someone small and wretched and totally alone. Each morning, I got out of bed feeling encompassed by darkness, and the shadows followed me throughout the day. Nights were unbearable. I stared into the actual darkness, knowing that my inner darkness was just as deep and black.

"Snap out of it!" I whispered to myself.

But I couldn't. The darkness seemed endless. Lying in my bed, I remembered crawling through the dark tunnel with Champion, but at least then I had held a candle in my hand—and I had caught a glimpse of the light that waited in the chamber ahead. I could see no light now. If I had, I would have directed my efforts toward that light—but I was blind.

Dark nights of the soul, I know now, would not be truly dark if we could see the way out of them. We must reach the point where we believe the darkness will last forever. We must allow ourselves to be content with darkness, to accept it. "If you sit in the darkness long enough," someone told me once, "eventually you make friends with it." I can't claim to have achieved a sense of friendship with darkness, but I did finally let go of my insistence that we *deserve* light. We must surrender.

And there at last we find God's will. But to our surprise, God's will coincides with our own deepest desires. We step into the light, and the Divine voice and our own become one.

With hindsight, I recognize the gifts these soul-nights bring, gifts of freedom and liberation. Jung would say that in the Shadow we are set free from our own egos with all their compulsions, paranoia, and insecurities. Saint John of the Cross put the same concepts in the language of Christianity: "The eternal fountain is hidden in the Living Bread that gives us being, even in the night." Rumi, the Sufi poet, wrote, "Life's waters flow from darkness.

Search the darkness, don't run from it." The darkness will eventually allow us to fulfill the true purposes for which we were born. We learn to relegate our false selves to the back seat, while we surrender to the Divinity that dwells within our own hearts.

Black nights of the soul are not, however, one-shot deals. They recur. John of the Cross wrote that after "periods of relief, the soul suffers once again, more intensely and keenly than before. . . . The fire of love goes deeper, to that falseness which is still more deeply rooted in the soul." Each time I have gone through one of these spiritual nights, my despair seems greater, my confusion more absolute. I never seem to learn. And yet, each time, sooner or later, I am surprised to find myself entering a period of new growth, understanding, and joy.

This time, in the weeks after my return from the Holy Land, what finally emerged from the darkness was a new clarity: I needed to leave the Abode. I had made wonderful friends—but whatever had been accomplished during my time here had now ended. It was time to go.

I rented a moving van and made my way back to New York City.

15

In the fire of the Divine love, I saw a whole universe,
and each particle was alive with the breath of Jesus.

Rumi

Jesus is revealed in every face,
sought in every sign . . .
worshiped in all that is truly loved,
and pursued in both the visible world
and the invisible.

Ibn 'Arabi

I thought things would get better now, that the darkness would finally give way to the dawn. I was wrong. There was still more ego that needed to be burned in the darkness before I could emerge into a period of light.

The Sufi leadership had chosen me to head their Manhattan center, and I left the Abode thinking I would go to that position. I suppose I expected this new role to define me now. But once again I was grasping at emptiness—and I soon realized that things had changed drastically at the Sufi center since I had last been there.

During my time away, the Manhattan Sufis had decided they didn't need a leader. They wanted a more democratic approach, where groups of people provided leadership instead of a single person. I took it personally, as a rejection of me. I was crushed.

Meanwhile, I was staying with my parents. My daughters were now on the other side of the country, and I felt as though I had come full circle. I was right back in the small, dark world I had worked so hard to escape.

My parents had been delighted when I left the Abode and returned to live with them, but their pleasure didn't last long. After all, a middle-aged daughter who had to live with her parents did nothing to prove their worth. As the weeks slipped by, I sensed their restlessness. I knew it was only a matter of time before their pleasure transformed itself into impatience and then resentment.

One morning at breakfast my mother looked up from her toast and said to me, "Oh, how I wish this had never happened. Your life would have been so different if you had never gone to that place. I don't know why this had to happen. I don't know why you *let* it happen!"

I set down my coffee cup and struggled to be calm. "Mom, listen to me," I said after I had counted to ten several times. "I'm trying the best I can. I'm sending out résumés every day. And I just got offered a sub job at a home for children with emotional problems—"

She interrupted before I could finish. "You had it so good, Marietta, better than most. Why did you have to throw it all away?"

I picked up my coffee cup again, took a sip, counted to ten one more time. "Look, Mom, going on like this isn't helping you or me—"

She leaned toward me and interrupted me again. "I don't understand you." Her voice was a whisper, her face as stricken as if I'd slapped her.

I sighed. *You never have,* were the words that hovered on my tongue. *Why should that be any different now?* I bit back the words. *One, two, three, four, five, six, seven, eight, nine, ten.* "No, I suppose you don't."

The look on her face made me want to comfort her, despite my exasperation. As I looked into her dark eyes, I was filled with a hopeless yearning. If only, just once, she could understand me.

I might as well have wished for roses to grow in a swamp.

That night, after one of my mother's homemade pasta dinners, my father finished his third glass of wine and then poured himself a glass of Sambuca. As he picked up the glass, he glanced across the table—and for a moment, he looked surprised, as though he had just noticed that his adult daughter was sitting at the table with him. "So." He cleared his throat, then took a swallow of the colorless liqueur. "What have you been doing with your days?"

"What have I been doing?" I heard my voice rise on the question, and I knew I was responding with an adolescent's sullen defensiveness. But I couldn't help myself. "I've been busy typing résumés, more than forty of them. I've sent them out to practically every school district in New York, plus a couple in Pennsylvania. And meanwhile, I'll be subbing at a school for children with emotional problems."

He snorted, as though I had said something funny. "Children with emotional problems? So this is what you've been reduced to? You had it so good, and now look at you."

"I had it good?" I wasn't going to bother counting to ten this time. "When, exactly, was that, Dad? You know better."

My father took another sip of his drink. "All I know," he said, "is that you had a successful husband, a house, a career, three beautiful children—if that wasn't having it good, I don't what is. And now, you have nothing. You threw it all away, and now you're right back where you started."

"Do you really know me so little, Dad?" I blurted. "You still don't comprehend that I'm headed in a different direction."

He tipped back his head and stared at me for a moment. "Direction?" His expression as he spoke the word would have shriveled the queen of England in her tracks. "Is that what you call it? *Direction?* At your age? Wake up, woman! You're not twelve years old, you know. It's about time you acted your age."

"Then stop treating me as if I were a child!" My voice was shrill. "And don't call me 'woman'! I have a name!"

He snickered. "Yeah, you do. And you've disgraced that name. You've disgraced us, your mother and me."

"This isn't about you," I shrieked. "This is about me and my life."

"Then why are you sitting at my table, eating my food?"

My mother jumped up. "Stop it, stop it!" she screamed. "The neighbors—the windows are open!" She rushed to the windows and slammed them shut.

I didn't know whether to laugh or cry.

My mother stood at the window for a moment longer, her shoulders heaving, and then she turned around and faced me across the table. "We sacrificed everything to send you to Catholic schools all your life," she said. "You had a good education. And now you've thrown it all away because you believe in a different God."

I sighed. "Oh, Mom, that's simply not true." I was starting to cry, but I ignored the tears running from my eyes. "It's the same God, believe me. If you would—"

"No," she interrupted. "It's *not* the same God. You were brought up to believe in Jesus Christ. Now you believe in a Sufi."

"No, Mom." I found myself laughing through my tears. "It's not *a* Sufi. Sufi is just the name for a group of people who worship God in a certain way. They—"

"They don't worship *my* God. Not the God we raised you to worship. Not the God *we* worship."

I put my hand up to my mouth to hide my smirk. My parents never went to church, they hadn't in years, so I wasn't sure exactly what God she was talking about.

"Sufi!" My father slammed his empty glass onto the

table. "A bunch of hippies living on a farm. When we visited you, they all looked as if they were on drugs! A bunch of men and women wearing dresses, twirling in circles. What kind of worship is that? I couldn't believe my daughter would have any part of it! It makes me ashamed. I'll never tell the family, you can be sure of that. They'd think you were crazy." He leaned back and sighed. "I'm not so sure they'd be wrong."

Without another word, I stood up from the table, went to my room, and started to pack.

After a few minutes of furious activity, I dropped down on my bed. I stared at myself in the mirror and faced the truth. Where could I go? I had no money. My parents were right: I had thrown everything away. I tried to speak my denial out loud, but I couldn't get the words out. Even though I was alone in my room, I was gagged, mute.

The only voice I heard coming from within me now was filled with scorn. "See?" it whispered. "You couldn't make it at the Abode, and you can't make it here. And for this you gave up everything! Now you have nothing. No job, no money. No friends, no home. What's left? And you thought you were so smart, so pure, so saintly!" On and on the voice chattered, a relentless, nagging mutter that echoed my parents' voices.

I signed up for more substitute teaching jobs, the only way I knew to make some money, hoping I would soon be able to move into my own apartment.

***

And then one afternoon, after a grueling day of teaching inner-city kids, a strange sensation washed over me, as though I were being pulled toward something familiar. The feeling was nearly tangible, as though a physical force were drawing me irresistibly forward, and yet the sensation was accompanied by neither images nor ideas. I discounted it as my imagination.

I forgot about the odd feeling until it occurred again. And then again. Each time, it was simply a blind sensation of both movement and familiarity. Each time, I discounted it as a trick of my imagination.

I kept discounting it until I could no longer ignore it. *What exactly is going on?* I asked myself. *The Manhattan Sufi center has practically shut down, I have no money, I'm a grown woman living with my parents, and I can't find a permanent teaching job. My life is a mess. I can't even pray. So what am I being pulled toward?*

I didn't know where to turn for answers. The Sufi practices I had done for years left me feeling empty now. Zikr was impossible. In desperation, I attempted the long-ago prayers of the Catholic Church but to no avail. I wanted . . . *something* . . .

What I wanted, I finally discovered, was to simply sit and be quiet: no words, no dancing, no bowing of my head, no reciting the rosary, nothing. Just quiet. I found peace in the quiet.

"Heck," said the scornful voice in my head. "Everybody knows that quiet is peaceful. It's not prayer. It's just relaxation."

And yet I was drawn again and again to the stillness and silence, as though it were the destination I was being pulled toward. The quiet welcomed me. It felt like home.

"What a waste of time!" the voice in my head told me. "Get busy. Do something!"

Then I came across these words, written by John of the Cross in a book called *Ascent of Mount Carmel*:

> *If you want to be truly spiritual, stop trying to achieve anything with your intellect, your senses, or any of your other faculties. Instead, become engrossed in one pure act—a calm state of rest and interior quiet. You will find the soul naturally wants to remain in that wordless peace as its proper place, its home. Since people do not understand the mystery of this new experience, however, they imagine themselves to be idle, doing nothing. You must learn to abide in the stillness with a loving attentiveness to God. At this stage, the faculties are at rest; they do not work actively but passively. They are open, receiving what God is accomplishing in them.*

If I could no longer pray in the usual ways, was it because God was calling me to something different, the sort of prayer Saint John had described? I knew enough about the saints and mystics to know that what I was experiencing might be some form of contemplative prayer: prayer emptied of thoughts, images, even emotions—but not love. But why did it feel so familiar, as though an old friend were gently nudging me closer? I had never experienced this sort of thing; it was the type of prayer done in contemplative orders and in monasteries.

In other words, it was *Catholic.*

I am not, I told myself, *returning to the Church!* I decided to ignore the whole thing.

Meanwhile, I was fortunate enough to get my old teaching job back. Finally, I could afford to leave my parents' home. With a huge sense of relief, I found a renovated carriage house to rent in Douglaston, New York, twenty minutes from the high school where I worked and a half hour from the beach where I loved to walk. I was overjoyed to be living alone again. No parents to answer to, no community's rules to obey. Middle-aged though I was, I felt like a young adult who is finally free and independent.

And I loved my new home. The kitchen was no more than the length and width of an elevator, so that the refrigerator had to be placed at the entry to the living room, and the bedroom was downstairs, a couple of feet below ground level, but none of that bothered me. The carriage house was perched among trees with windows on three sides of the living room. Sitting there, surrounded by leaves and light, I had the feeling I was living in a tree house.

I immersed myself in teaching and making new friends; for several months, I had no time to think about the spiritual life. Now and then, I attended Sufi conferences or got together with my Sufi friends, but neither activity pulled at my soul, calling me deeper.

And then I found myself becoming fascinated with Teresa of Avila, the great sixteenth-century saint. As I read about her, I learned that even though she was a nun, she had avoided prayer until she was in her forties. At that point, a priest convinced her to go back to her prayer, but she still found it hard work. She wrote, "I was more anxious for the hour of prayer to be over than I was to remain there. . . . This intellect is so wild that it doesn't seem to be anything else than a frantic madman no one can tie down."

I knew exactly how she felt! But Teresa persevered until finally she could write these words:

> Mental prayer in my opinion is nothing else than an intimate sharing between friends. It means taking time frequently to be alone with the One who we know loves us. The important thing is not to think much but to love much and do that which best stirs you to love. Love is not so much an emotion of joy but a desire to please God in everything.

In Teresa's books, she analyzes and dissects her mystical experiences the way a scientist would. I fell in love with her, and I longed to become a contemplative like her.

But I didn't know how to go about it. I made a tiny prayer space in a closet with a kneeler and a small table as an altar. I knelt there each day after school, eyes closed, trying hard to concentrate on God. Instead, thoughts ran through my head like Teresa's "frantic madman."

In the rare moments when I was alone in my little tree house, however, not thinking about anything in particular, that familiar gentle wave washed over me again and again, edging me into silence, peace, rest. *What is going on?* I asked myself—but then the phone would ring or it would be time to go to work, and I would once again push the odd sensation out of my consciousness.

And then one night as I lay in bed, about to close my eyes, the silent, imageless wave began to assume a shape. It was the oddest experience, as though I were staring at a cloud's hazy form, only to find it gathering itself together into something solid . . .

I was looking at the shape of a cross, I realized.

I couldn't sleep. Instead, I sat in bed, pondering why this shape seemed so firm and definite in my mind's eye. What was my unconscious saying to me? I felt as though I were continuing to be drawn slowly, gently toward something—something familiar and well-loved.

"No!" I whispered in response. "I will not go back to the Church!"

No, came the silent answer. *Not the Church.*

"Well, what then?" Feeling cross and confused, I finally fell asleep.

In the weeks that followed, the visual shape of a cross haunted me with an ever-greater intensity. I wanted to ignore it. What could it mean except a return to the

Church I had worked so hard to leave? Was I saying farewell to Sufism? Would I be asked to debunk all I had learned? Start all over again? I felt exhausted and overwhelmed just thinking about it.

Yet the feeling persisted. I yearned to know what it meant.

As I have so often done in my life when seeking answers, I turned to academia. I enrolled in a master's program at the Immaculate Conception Seminary in Huntington, Long Island, not knowing if I even wanted another degree. What I wanted was to learn more about this guy who had lived nearly two thousand years ago—so naturally, my first course was in Christology. If Jesus Christ was nudging his way into my life, then I had to get to know him in a new way, a way removed from the traditional theology of my childhood that had taught me only guilt and death.

My first class did give me a hint of something different. I caught a glimpse of a Jesus I had not imagined. As time went on, I had the sense that I was befriending a real person, a Jesus far different from the one I had heard preached at Sunday Mass. The Jesus I was coming to know was filled with magnanimity and abundance.

This Jesus rejoiced in his Father's providence. Unlike his precursor, the ascetic John the Baptist, who fasted and preached repentance, Jesus ate, drank, danced, and was shockingly extravagant. His first miracle was at a party—a wedding—where the host had run out of wine. Jesus not only turned water into wine, but he also made sure the new wine was better than the previous one.

Water into wine. The story pulled at my imagination. Did it mean—could it possibly mean?—that Jesus wanted to transform my colorless, bland life into something rich-hued and flavorful, something intoxicating? The idea was like no Christian theology I had ever heard.

I found Christ's extravagance revealed in story after story. When the woman with the alabaster jar poured expensive ointment over his feet, the disciples complained that the ointment was worth a year's wages that could be more sensibly spent—but Jesus honored the woman's gift and told his disciples to leave her alone. When he multiplied the loaves and fishes, the feast was far more than enough to feed those present. In the parable Jesus told about the prodigal son, he said that the father not only forgave the rebellious young man but also welcomed him with open arms and threw him a lavish party. And in another of Christ's parables, he described a Samaritan who rescued a wounded man and then put him up in an inn and paid all his expenses. All these Gospel accounts revealed to me an outrageously generous Christ who delighted in Divine providence—and in giving it all away.

This was the Jesus I was coming to know. He was still a savior, but not in the way I had grown up thinking of him. Instead, this savior had come to rescue us from our terrible brokenness, from our tendency to war and crime, to racism and sexism and all the other isms, to fear and poverty. Saint Paul wrote that Christ became sin for us (2 Corinthians 5:21), that he "emptied himself" and became one of us (Philippians 2:7)—and now I understood these verses in a new and startling way. Christ's greatest anguish on the cross had been his experience of our separation from God. Until then, he had lived as we are each intended to live, in loving and intimate harmony with his Father, but now he took our alienation from God into his own dying flesh.

Love by its very nature gives itself away—and God is love. I had grown up with the image of a bloody, dying man on a cross as the central symbol of the Christian faith, but now I came to believe that even if the cross had not been necessary, the Incarnation would still have happened—because God is recklessly, wildly generous, giving God-Self to Creation endlessly, humbly, tenderly. Contrary to what I had been taught all my life, Jesus' mission on Earth had nothing to do with guilt and morality. He had come for one reason only: to bring God's love to us, through his own human flesh.

I was stunned, awed, overwhelmed.

I was falling in love.

How could the Church have reduced this astonishing message of utter love to a list of do's and don'ts? Down through the ages, I knew, the saints and mystics had seen deeper and truer, but most of us sitting in the pews had heard only a constant message of guilt and fear, a message that hammered away at our souls, opening our inner gates to self-hatred and despair.

Even when I had heard God's love preached from the pulpit, it had been insipid, passionless. The Sufis worshipped with an ecstatic tenderness I had never glimpsed in Christianity, but now I saw in Jesus the Beloved, the One I had yearned for in the zikr, the One who had made me dance and whirl and filled my heart with joy.

I no longer wanted to plod through life, struggling endlessly to do right. I wanted to abandon myself to love. I wanted to let myself burn with Christ's fire. "We are put on earth a little space," William Blake wrote, "that we may learn to bear the beams of love." This was what I wanted now, I told myself.

All that sounded so good. Like the spokes of a wheel reaching out from its center into different directions, so had been the course of my life—but now, surely, I had found my place at the center of the turning wheel. Finally, I assured myself, I had discovered the answer to all my life's questions. If I still felt uncomfortable whenever I looked at a crucifix or some other image of Jesus, I shrugged off the sensation and paid it no attention. I was drunk on new ideas, intoxicated by theology.

After three years of seminary, I earned a Master of Theology. When I retired from teaching, I told myself, my degree would be my entry into church ministry. I could easily picture what I would have to offer in that role. I was eager to share all I had learned.

I had patted and stroked my ego into a slightly different shape, but my false self was alive and well. As always,

I was using my "spirituality" as a way to be seen, a way to be heard—but it was still my ego doing all the talking. Meanwhile, my true self was silent, still waiting.

God is patient, though, and the Divine was not done with me yet. In the years ahead, God's providence surprised and delighted me again and again with its extravagance.

16

Love gave birth to us.
Love is our mother. . . .
Don't grieve.
Love always comes back to you
in another form
Rumi

One of the biggest surprises was that my mother and I became friends.

We went out to lunch together, we went shopping, we visited my aunts. After work, I would call her on the phone, and we chatted for hours like schoolgirls. She listened and sympathized while I complained about problem students, the school administration, and money. We laughed together.

It seemed like a miracle. I had never believed my mother could show me a different side of herself. I had never thought I would feel her love the way I did now. Her given name—Lucy, a name from the Latin word *lux*—took on a new meaning for me. For the first time, my mother brought light to my life.

If my mother could be transformed from the terrifying witch of my childhood into a loving mother, than anything might happen. Life seemed full of intoxicating possibilities.

Then one wintry Sunday afternoon in February, the phone rang. "Marietta!" said my father's voice. "You need to come quickly!"

My mother's angina had suddenly worsened. The doctor wanted to perform surgery as quickly as possible. An ambulance was on its way to my parent's house.

I hurried to their house and found my mother dressing to leave for the hospital. She sat down on the bed and looked up at me, her dark eyes filled with something I had never seen there.

"Will you help me?" she asked. I saw the muscles in her throat move as she swallowed, and then she said, "I need you to—I can't tie my shoes. Will you help me?"

"Of course, Mom." She had never before asked me to do anything for her, not something so small and intimate. I knelt and bent over her feet, tying the laces on first one shoe and then the other. I made tight, neat bows, and then I lifted my head. "Don't worry, Mom. Once this operation is over, you'll feel like your old self again." She smiled down at me, a soft smile only for me.

She said nothing, though. The ambulance arrived then, and the moment passed.

As the paramedics bent over my mother, one of them said, "What a beautiful home you have, ma'am!"

My mother smiled again. I knew her home was her pride and joy, the only creative work she had ever been allowed.

My father and I followed the ambulance to the hospital. When my mother was wheeled into the emergency room, she was no longer calm and smiling. Instead, she clutched at her chest, clearly in agony. I snatched her handbag off the stretcher and began to rummage for her pills, hoping to relieve her pain—but she reached up and grabbed her handbag from my hands.

"Stop!" she screamed.

Startled, I stared down into her face. Her black eyes glared up at me from her white face. She looked as accusing as if I had been about to give her poison.

"What were you thinking?" she gasped through her pain. "Don't you know they'll take away the medication if they see it? I may need them!"

"But you're in pain now!" I protested. With one part of my brain, I was my grown-up self who knew my mother was hurting too much to be rational, but at the same moment, I was also suddenly the long-ago little girl, standing in the white kitchen, paralyzed with fear by those dark, dark eyes.

I turned away, shaking.

I went back to my parents' house and prepared dinner for my father. Then I called the hospital and spoke to my mother one last time.

"We'll be there tomorrow," I told her. "Nicky, Dad, and I will see you before you go into surgery."

"All right." Her voice was weak and faraway.

"Rest tonight. Don't worry. Promise me, Mom?"

"Yes," she said softly. "I promise." And then she hung up.

I went back to my own home, but at midnight the phone rang. My mother had died of a massive heart attack.

I dressed quickly and drove to the Bronx to be with my father. I suppose I thought he would need me to comfort him, but when I arrived, he said, "I'm going to bed. It's too late to notify anyone now."

After he had gone into the bedroom, I sat alone in the living room. I knew I would not sleep. I picked up my mother's rosary and tried to pray, but behind my closed eyelids, I saw black eyes glaring at me. *You're a bad little girl,* I heard a long-ago voice say.

What I had always feared had happened: my mother had abandoned me forever.

✳✳✳

I missed her terribly during the months that followed. Finally, a year later, I decided to distract myself from my grief by traveling to Italy with some Sufi friends.

As we walked the busy streets and explored ancient cities, I felt again and again as if someone other than my friends were walking beside me. Each time I turned around, it was as if someone were turning with me. The invisible presence comforted me.

Then one day, my friends and I noticed a church perched on a hill in the distance. "Let's go there!" I said on impulse.

But the others were happy to continue shopping, and so I told them I would meet them later. I set off on my own toward the church.

At last, I climbed the hill and went inside. Everything glistened, and the silence seemed to welcome me. I sat down in a pew—and then, without warning, I began to cry.

A priest came toward me down the aisle, but when I covered my face with my hands, he must have decided to leave me alone. My tears were like a storm sweeping through me. My shoulders heaved, and I sobbed out loud.

Finally, the tears subsided. I sat quietly for a while, then wiped my face and rose to leave. As I stood up, I glanced up at the wall encircling the choir loft, and for the first time, I saw the name of the church: Saint Lucy's.

Lucy, the saint who is connected to vision and the coming of light. Lucy, my mother.

Maybe she hadn't abandoned me after all.

For just a moment, I was sure I breathed the scent of roses.

✳✳✳

Life is filled with mystery. I had not yet come to terms with the meaning of my own voice—but I was truly seeing life in new ways. Light was shining into the dark corners, taking me by surprise again and again.

Two years after my mother's death, someone I had known since the first grade came back into my life. Bill and I had gone to grade school together, and then, years later, we went on a single date while we were both attending Fordham University. I had not seen him for many years, but now he had organized a reunion for our elementary school. At the reunion, Bill and I renewed our friendship.

Then, one Sunday afternoon, I heard a knock on my front door. When I opened the door, there stood Bill.

17

Your task is not to seek for love,
but merely to seek and find all the barriers within yourself
that you have built against it.
Rumi

"What are you doing here?" I blurted.

"I've just come from seeing Ed." Ed was a mutual friend, another of our old classmates. "I was on my way home upstate, but first, I decided to look you up. So here I am."

Indeed, here he was. I looked at him—his gray-brown curly locks, his broad shoulders, his wide green eyes—and I smiled. I remembered those eyes from elementary school; he was both familiar to me and at the same time, someone utterly new. I swung the door open wider to let him come in.

"So are you still teaching?" I asked as we sat down. At the reunion, I had learned that he, like me, taught English at a high school.

"Yes, still teaching. Loving every minute of it."

"I wish I could say the same." I sighed. "I'm afraid I've lost interest. Kids don't seem to care about learning the way they did once. And of course, we're having the usual problems with drugs. Is it the same upstate?"

We talked for quite some time about the status of education in a changing world, but all the while, I sensed something else beneath our conversation, a deep, fast-moving current that made me shiver with excitement.

Finally, Bill asked, "Have you had dinner?"

I shook my head.

He smiled. "So where's a good place to eat around here?"

I gathered up my coat and bag, and off we went. The fast current I had sensed had swept me up and was bearing me forward. I could not tell where it would take me, but I was invigorated and unafraid.

Bill called me the following week, and again the next week and the week after that. He seemed to be finding lots of reasons to travel from upstate New York downstate. Soon, we were spending all our weekends together. When summer arrived, we took long walks on Jones Beach. We shared hot dogs and ice cream cones. We talked about our lives. I was supremely happy with him, and I missed him terribly each time he had to leave.

I knew that not everyone understood or was comfortable with Bill. He was brutally honest, fiercely loyal, and uncompromisingly just. He challenged hypocrisy wherever he encountered it. Never before had I known a man with such purity of soul. He loved me unconditionally, in a way I had never experienced. How could I resist?

And yet I stumbled over the practical details. We lived hundreds of miles away from each other; if we wanted to be together, one of us would need to move. Should I retire? Should he retire? Should I move upstate? Should he move downstate? I fretted over the questions.

"Look," Bill said, "don't do anything you don't want to do. Give yourself time."

"Okay," I agreed—but then I'd bring up the questions all over again.

"If you want," he promised, "I'll retire and move down here to Long Island."

"Retire?" I threw up my hands. "You can't retire! You love teaching too much. Besides, you couldn't stand the traffic on the Island. It would drive you crazy. You would hate living here."

"Probably. But you're worth the sacrifice." He was calm, determined, relentless.

"Oh, stop it! I can't have you doing that." I would have to leave my little tree house near the beach, I decided.

"You have nothing to say about it," he said. "I make my own decisions."

We decided to check out a couple of houses in Sag Harbor, my favorite place on Long Island. The prices were way outside our budget, though, even for houses that needed lots of work. Something told me this wasn't the right path for us.

"Don't be so quick to give up!" Bill insisted.

"I see the reality of the situation!"

"You never see the reality of anything! Your head is always in the clouds, pondering some deep theological question." He grinned. "Maybe that's why I love you so much."

The man was incorrigible. But I couldn't feel the same certainty he did. I knew I loved him. But should I marry him?

✳✳✳

Finally, I decided to visit a Dominican Mother House, where one of my nun friends lived. My friend was busy, so I slipped into the chapel, thinking I might find my answers there.

I sat in a pew, but I couldn't pray. A statue of Jesus stood to my right, but I could not bring myself to look at it. I stared straight ahead, my anxiety and confusion screaming silently inside me. *Can you hear me, Jesus? Can you hear me? Can you?*

I don't know how long I sat there in the chapel's still-ness. All I remember is that I felt as though something was wrapped tight around my chest, shutting off my breath, clutching at my heart. Beads of sweat rolled from my hairline and down my forehead. "Help me!" I finally gasped past the constriction in my chest. "Tell me what to do! I think I love him—but is that enough?"

The silence within the chapel continued. It offered me no answer to my desperate questions. Finally, feeling drained and weak, I rose to leave. As I did, I still kept my gaze turned away from the statue of Jesus. I started to leave the chapel, hoping my friend would have time to talk with me now.

And then I hesitated. I stood still for a moment, facing the door. Finally, I turned around and looked at the statue of Jesus. I met its stone gaze . . .

Slowly, slowly, a feeling of peace swept over me, enveloped me. I sighed. All my tension flowed out of me.

I turned back to the chapel door. By the time I went outside, I was convinced: I was going to marry Bill.

✳✳✳

But my sense of certainty was fleeting. Once I was back home, I wondered if it had all been my imagination, and I was again tossed and tormented by indecision. Meanwhile, the time was fast approaching when I had to make a decision. We couldn't go on as we were, separated by hundreds of miles. Either I had to make a commitment, or we'd have to separate.

I was frightened. For years now, I had told myself my life was dedicated to God, that I was on a spiritual quest, and that I would never remarry. I had even entertained the thought of joining a religious order. Should I stay true to those convictions and say good-bye to Bill?

Was that what I wanted?

Was it what God wanted?

I was utterly confused. I needed discernment.

Discernment? The word caught my attention. I knew from my theological studies that the word "discern" was an important one to Ignatius of Loyola, the sixteenth-century founder of the Jesuits. Loyola was famous for initiating a method of discernment both for himself and his priests. Down through the centuries since then, the Church had used his method to discern the presence of "good and bad spirits."

At the seminary, I had met a nun, Sister Josephine, who had mentioned to me that she gave Ignatian retreats.

I had to do something. I picked up the phone and called Sister Josephine.

18

When you have found the courage
to marry forgiveness,
when you have found the courage
to marry love,
the sun will stand up with you at the wedding,
whistling.

Hafiz

A few days later, I found myself once more outside a door, hesitating, scared to go inside. What else did God have for me to learn? How would this new adventure change me? What answers would I find? I wasn't sure what I hoped for. Did I want to regain that sense of calm I had felt at the Dominican Mother House chapel, the absolute certainty that marriage to Bill was the right path for me? Or was I hoping I would somehow be freed to return to my old life before Bill had burst into my heart?

I sucked in a deep breath, squared my shoulders, and knocked on the door.

Sister Josephine ushered me into her study. Wall-to-wall bookshelves lined the room. I noticed that photographs of Italy, France, and Spain hung on any space not occupied by bookshelves, and a vase of red and white tulips was on a side table. Curtains the color of peaches hung at the window.

Josephine motioned me to sit in a huge leather chair across from her even more immense desk. I settled into the chair, feeling very small,

"Well," she asked, once she had taken her seat behind the desk, "just exactly why do you want to make the retreat?"

"Because I need to discern what I should do," I said.

She smiled. "Well, yes, that is the usual reason for the Ignatian retreat—discernment. But just what sort of discernment are you looking for?"

I gulped, then plunged in. "I'm at wit's end. I no longer know what I want in my life. I know I want to devote my life to God—but now this man—Bill—has come into my life and—he wants to marry me. I just don't know. I—" I looked down at my lap, at my hands that were curled into tight fists. After a moment, I looked up again and met her kind, level gaze. "I simply don't know what to do, Sister."

"Why can't you devote your life to God *and* marry Bill?" she asked. "Does one exclude the other?"

"Well, it shouldn't . . . but I just don't know . . . I don't know if they would even accept me into a religious order!"

"Religious order?" She raised her eyebrows. "Where did that come from? What religious order?"

"Oh. . ." I looked back at my hands again. "None in particular. It was just a thought!" I sucked in a shaky breath. "I don't know!"

"Calm down," she replied, "and stop saying 'I don't know.' You sound like you're about fourteen—and you're not!" Josephine was never one to mince words.

"Okay." I drew in another breath and tried to calm myself.

She looked at me for a moment with her steady brown eyes, and then she said, "You're doing the right thing, Bahri. The Ignatian retreat is perfect for discernment with issues like yours. Besides, I haven't given one in a long time." Her mouth softened into an impish grin. "It will be fun. I look forward to the adventure."

Some adventure, I thought to myself.

"So let's get started," she said. "What do you know about Ignatius of Loyola?"

I thought I knew plenty. After all, I had graduated from Fordham University, where I'd been taught by Jesuits. I had a degree in theology. But Josephine waved away all my claims to knowledge. "What do you know about the man? About what he taught?"

"I suppose," I said, feeling a little deflated, "well, I guess I know only that the Jesuits are rather liberal. They focus on education and missions. . . ." I shrugged. "That's about all I know."

She nodded. "That's what I thought. Not that you actually need to know anything about Ignatius for a successful retreat. But getting to know the man might help you broaden your vision—and gain more clarity."

I wasn't convinced. How could a man from the sixteenth century help me with my twentieth-century dilemma? I was too polite to say that, though, so I asked her to tell me more.

Her knowing glance told me she guessed my thoughts. "I'll try to make it short." She settled back in her chair and began her story.

Ignatius, I learned, had been a Spanish nobleman, born in 1491. In young adulthood, he devoted himself both to a military career and to the pursuit of a noble young woman. Then, during a battle in northern Spain, a cannonball broke his leg, and he was sent home to the family castle to recover. He wanted desperately for his lady to see him as a "whole" man, so he forced his doctors to operate, thinking they could repair his leg. He endured three operations, performed without anesthesia, but to no avail. His leg was still crippled.

The boredom of being confined to his bed forced him to ask a female attendant to bring him books. He had requested romances, tales of chivalry and heroism, but she was a pious woman, and she brought him instead two books that would forever change his life. The first one was the Gospels, and the second was written by a bishop of the Middle Ages, Jacques de Voragine. In it, Ignatius read about the conversion of great sinners who became champions of the Faith by fighting against heresy and all forms of evil.

Ignatius longed to imitate these saints—and yet he also longed for the pleasures and comforts to which he was accustomed. The two sets of longing pulled at him from opposite directions, jerking him first one direction and than another. Torn, anguished, he felt as though his soul was swinging back and forth.

Then, slowly, he began to notice something: when his consciousness swayed in one direction, he experienced a sense of peace and resolve. When he felt himself swing in the opposite direction, however, he felt troubled and sad. He turned his attention to analyzing the sense of movement from one direction to another. The sense of swaying between opposite poles, he realized, was actually a flow of thoughts, images, emotions, and subtle sensations. At last, he concluded that when his soul moved in one particular direction, he was experiencing the peace of aligning his will with God's. He resolved to commit his life to serving God.

This experience formed the foundation for his thoughts on the discernment process. But he took it even further. When he had finally recovered from his injury, he left the comfort of his home, and for eight months, he lived as a hermit in a cave. He spent this time immersed in prayer, all the while clarifying the discernment process as he came to experience it. Out of this was born his Spiritual Exercises. These also became the foundation for the Jesuit Order.

Ignatius then visited the Holy Land, and upon his return to Spain, he gave the Spiritual Exercises to anyone who would listen to them. Going from city to city, he ran into the Spanish Inquisition and was repeatedly brought to trial. Although he was acquitted each time, he realized he needed to root his exercises now in a deeper understanding of theology. He completed theological studies in Paris in 1534—and then he formed the nucleus of the Society of Jesus.

"That's how it all began," Josephine finished. "So you see—you are not the first to be faced with a seemingly unsolvable spiritual dilemma. Nor will you be the last."

I thought about Ignatius' story. I suspected his exercises would guide me toward abandoning any "worldly" romantic relationship so that I could commit myself more deeply to spiritual matters. After all, that was the route Ignatius had taken. As I pondered this, I felt both a sense of resistance—and relief.

"So," I said at last, "how long does the retreat take?"

"There are various ways to do an Ignatian retreat," Josephine answered. "In your case, you'll come once a week for a period of nine months. Each week, you'll read what Ignatius has to say about the life of Christ. Then you will write how you feel your life may reflect Christ's life. You will take note of what troubles you in your life presently—conflicts, sadness—as well as what brings you joy. Then you will bring your journal here, and we will discuss what you have written." She handed me a slim book that bore the title *The Book of Exercises*.

I looked down at the book in my hand. Somehow, I had expected it to be something more physically substantial. What could this little book have to offer my situation. "And that's it?" I asked.

Josephine raised her brows. "What more did you expect?"

"Well. . ." I started to say, *I don't know*, but I caught myself in time. "What if I can't see how my life reflects Christ?" I asked. "What do I write then? Where do I find the answers? Where do I start?" I felt like a freshman college student who had been given her first major writing assignment.

Josephine smiled. "This isn't something you can get wrong, Bahri. It's not a test. There are no grades. It's simply a matter of trust."

"Trust?"

She nodded. "Your doubts and worries will come and go throughout the retreat. They don't matter. Ignore them as much as you can. Trust that you'll be guided. By something outside yourself. Trust that you do not embark on this retreat alone. The Holy Spirit goes with you—and longs to help you."

She got to her feet and held out her hand to me. I took it, thanked her, and said good-bye. I drove home in a fog of emotion, thinking back over her words. At last, when I pulled into my driveway, I let out a sigh. I felt the muscles in my neck and shoulders relax.

I was ready to trust.

✳✳✳

The retreat wasn't quite what I had expected. I had been looking for discernment for a specific dilemma, whether or not to marry Bill. Instead, one of the first things I discovered was an overwhelming, all-consuming awareness that I was completely forgiven.

Forgiven? For what? Those were my first questions in response to the sense of deep peace that washed over me. The answer came into my consciousness quietly but firmly: *Everything!*

Everything I had thought was dark, shameful, and irreparably damaged: my childhood failures and insecurities; the sense of guilt that drove me to the confessional for so many years when I was still a "good daughter" of the Church; my sense of rejection and anger related to Mary; the fury and hurt of my marriage to Pete; my distrust of people; my cowardice; my selfishness; my pettiness; all of it, every single, tiny shadow, had been transformed into light. I was free.

As I continued with the Ignatian retreat, I came to understand forgiveness in a new way. We don't receive Divine pardon because we are "bad," but so we can see ourselves in a new way, so we can begin anew with a clean slate. That pure, beautiful, and shining slate is what we are in God's eyes, beings of glowing potential. We are the ones who place judgments on ourselves; we are the ones who created words like "immoral" and "bad" in the first place, and then we project those concepts onto God. God does not judge.

But I had judged myself, harshly and cruelly down through the years of my life. Now I needed to forgive myself. Until I did, I could not be intimate with my own

deepest self—and if I could not achieve that most intimate of intimacies, I would never truly know God.

The Sufis had done their best to teach me this, but
apparently, I was ready now to grasp it differently, perhaps more deeply, within the framework of Christianity.
(So often I seem to have to relearn the same lessons again
and again!) Now, finally, I could let go of the past, including the failures of my marriage to Pete. I hadn't realized
I was still carrying the old weight of my marriage until I
felt it fall off me. I knew I could say yes to Bill.

Awestruck by all I was experiencing, I tried to describe
my thoughts to Josephine. I finished by saying, "It just
wasn't what I expected."

She smiled. "You sound surprised. What *did* you
expect?"

"Not this." I frowned, searching for words. "I mean,
well, it's not like I began the retreat thinking I needed
forgiveness. I wasn't aware that it was an issue for me.
I didn't know that it was what stood between me and
saying yes to Bill. And yet . . . it's like the retreat knew
exactly where to point me."

She continued to smile. "So you're finally finding out
about this God of ours. Good."

I felt a little offended. "What do you mean, 'finally
finding out'?" I protested. "I've been on a spiritual path for
years. I think I knew *something!*"

She nodded. "Of course you did. But sometimes we
need to let go of what we know or think we know. We

need to let God point out our blind spots. We need to
be open to surprise. Through the retreat, you are coming to know God in a new way. You are allowing your
knowledge to become deeper, closer, more intimate than
before. After all these years, you're finally ready to get
down to the nitty-gritty."

"'Finally'?" I protested again. "For goodness sake, Josephine, I've been through some pretty rough times."

She nodded. "True. You have. But the spiritual life is a
long and arduous voyage. It's as though up until now you
had only barely backed out of your driveway—and just
doing that took everything you had. Now, finally, you're
ready to start the actual journey. Who knows how long it
will last? I suspect most of us don't reach our destination
until the other side of the grave. If then."

I had a slight but very real urge to whack her smiling
face. "Thanks for the encouragement," I muttered.

"Oh just wait until you're a little further along," she
said. "Right now life is still full of excitement and possibility. Wait till you find out there's nowhere to go and
nothing to do. . . !"

I threw up my hands. "Enough! Damn it, Josephine,
you're supposed to help me, not throw a wet blanket
over me!"

"I am helping you." She put her arms around me.
"You'll understand some day."

Within the warm circle of her embrace, I suddenly
wanted to cry.

***

But the Ignatian retreat still had more to teach me. About halfway through it, I knew I had reached a turning point. I could go back to where I had been or go forward into an unknown—both literally and spiritually—where nothing would be the same again.

I mentioned this to Josephine.

"Close your eyes," she said. "Now tell me, what does this turning point look like?"

With my eyes shut, I evaluated my sense of where I stood. "I'm not sure. It has something to do with letting go of the false gods."

"Ah, false gods, And which ones would those be, in your case?"

"The ones I see now that I've been worshipping most of my life," I answered. "My parents, of course, but also my teachers, my education, my career. Even my ethnicity, my identification with certain groups, all my values that are based on a skewed idea of the world, a subtle sort of pride. And my obsession with my own neurosis, even that's a false god." I fell silent, my eyes still closed, and then I sighed and opened them. "That's about all I've come up with for now."

She nodded. "That's a good start. And where has the retreat pointed you through all this?"

"Toward Jesus," I said, certain of this answer at least. "I find myself identifying with how he must have felt when he left his home. Not knowing if he and his teaching would be accepted. Reaching out to those who couldn't understand him. In a way, turning his back on all he had known. He knew he had to leave his old way of living and not look behind him." I looked away from her knowing eyes and stared out her window. "I guess that's what I mean by reaching a turning point. I can't go back—and yet, I'm still terrified of going forward. I no longer have the old props to hold me up. I'm letting them go. When I marry Bill, I'll be going first to a geographical place I know nothing about—upstate New York—and then into a psychological space that may cripple me. But I can't turn back!"

Josephine pushed me to go further, saying, "What is it about the unknown that you fear most?"

"I'm not sure." I searched my heart for a moment, trying to identify the fear that lurked there in the shadows. At last, I said, "Loneliness."

"Even with Bill? I would think marriage would offer you protection against loneliness."

I shook my head. "It has nothing to do with being married. It's a kind of loneliness where I might not have the support I need for my feelings, my thoughts. It's a terrible dread that what I want will be ridiculed, laughed at. Considered plain nuts."

"As your parents sometimes ridiculed your beliefs and wishes?"

I nodded. "When I was with the Sufis, I received spiritual support for the first time in my life. I'm afraid I'll never have it again. I don't expect to find it in the Church, at least not in individual churches."

"And can you identify with Jesus even in this fear of loneliness?" she asked me.

I nodded again. "Jesus knew this loneliness. The Temple priests didn't understand him. They became suspicious of him, and they finally regarded him as their enemy. I don't think I'll be regarded as an enemy, I don't think I'm going to be put to death—but it's the same sort of feeling I'm talking about. Jesus was so alone. His closest friends turned away from him. They didn't get him!"

Josephine looked thoughtful. "You say you're not worried that you'll be put to death. But isn't that what really terrifies you? Not physical death. But something worse than just the fear of the unknown. Isn't it the threat of being 'crucified' in some way?"

Tears sprang to my eyes. "Yes," I whispered.

"Don't you think this terror is what Jesus also felt in Gethsemane when he prayed for strength to face his own death?"

"Yes, but Jesus had a handle on it. He knew what he was in for, at least he must have had a sense. But I don't even have that. I'm just so scared."

"Can you get into the consciousness of Jesus? Can you feel the way he felt, when he sweated blood?"

"No!" Identifying with Jesus was one thing, but this was going too far. "I can't do that! I'm not the Son of God!"

"I'm asking that you try to feel what he felt, though. Go with Jesus to Gethsemane. Allow yourself to be with him there." She stood up and put her hand on my shoulder. "Sit here alone for a few minutes. I'll go next door."

***

I tried hard, very hard, to do as Josephine had instructed. Nothing happened.

Just when I was about to give up, I felt as though a crack opened in my darkness, a crack that led to still deeper darkness, giving me a glimpse, only a glimpse, of the pain Jesus carried on his way to Calvary. That one brief vision, even if it was only my imagination, was enough to reach deep into me. I realized that Christ's pain was like mine, only magnified to infinity.

That was all I could do. It left me as enervated as if I had been doing hard physical work.

During the following weeks, though, my fears seemed to slowly evaporate. I found myself remembering a dream I'd had years before, long before I became a Sufi. In the dream, I saw faces looking into mirrors, faces that looked exactly alike, as though the same image was being reflected again and again, and yet I knew that each face was a different individual. Each face belonged to a different soul—and yet each face reflected the image of all the other faces. The dream had been bizarre, confusing, yet filled with a sense of joy. Now, for the first time, I felt I understood what it had been telling me.

My essence mirrors the essence of another; the essence of others mirrors my essence. Each of us holds up this mirror, despite our many differences in outward form. And if our essence is Divine, I realized, if, indeed,

God dwells within us at our deepest point, then it is the Divine image we see in each other—and in our own truest selves. God mirrors God-Self within us, so that who we truly are as individuals are Divine reflections, God living through us.

The implications of these thoughts astounded me. If human beings could look at each other this way, wouldn't war, poverty, competition, hatred, fear, prejudice, delusion, and all the other self-destructive tendencies of our lives disappear? We'd awaken to the true purpose of our existence.

But as every religious tradition claims, in order for this to happen we must "die." Die to who we think we are, and realize who we truly are. Our unbridled egos must undergo a painful but glorious transformation as we learn to surrender to the Divinity within. The way is not easy, yet it is the only path to both personal freedom and the kingdom of God.

The world was a far bigger place than I had ever imagined, filled with mysteries greater than I could comprehend. Instead of understanding things better, I seemed only to be more aware of all I did not know. But one thing had become certain: I could not turn my back on the love that Bill offered me. His unconditional love was the clearest mirror of Divine love I had ever found. Refusing to accept Bill's love would be like turning away from God. And it would be tantamount to condemning myself to an existence devoid of fullness and beauty.

And so, when the retreat was over, I decided to retire, move to upstate New York, and marry Bill. Once the decision was made, I was simply and deliriously happy.

***

My father did not share my joy. He adamantly opposed the marriage, casting a shadow over my happiness that felt all too familiar.

"Why are you doing this?" he cried when I gave him the news. "You always said you'd never marry again!"

"But, Dad," I replied, trying to keep my voice level, "I fell in love with this man."

He banged his hand on the kitchen table, a gesture so familiar, I didn't even flinch. "Love? That's what you said about your first husband! You're too old for such foolishness now. And to top all that, you're going where? To a place that's hundreds of miles away!"

I sucked in a deep breath and then replied as calmly as I could, "It's only three hours away. You could move too, so that you lived close to us."

My father's face turned red. "Why would I want to do that?" He screamed the words into my face. "I have your brother here, my friends are here. I've lived in the Bronx all my life, and now you want me to change? *What's wrong with you, woman?*"

This was exactly how he had spoken to my mother, the words a familiar refrain from all the years I had lived in their house: What's wrong with you, woman? For the first time, I found myself understanding my mother's sense of helplessness and humiliation.

All I could say was, "Will you at least come to the wedding?"

The anger slowly faded from his face. Now, he looked at me as if I had knifed him. "No." He spoke the single, soft word with total finality.

I ran from the apartment, down five flights of stairs, and got into my car. As I drove home, my hands shaking on the steering wheel, I kept asking myself: *Why does my father hate me?*

I knew my father had hoped I would move in with him—but instead I had found another husband, and I was moving away from the world he knew. My marriage to Bill threatened my father in a way I could only dimly understand.

He removed me from his will, and then he kept his promise: he did not come to our wedding.

***

We were married the day after Christmas in a small Episcopal church in Windsor, New York, a few miles from Bill's home. Snow shrouded the ground around the church and the surrounding mountains, and I shivered—but inside, the church glowed with the light of Christmas. Holly lined the stained glass windows and altar rails. A small crèche flanked the left side of the altar, and a regal old organ was on the right. A golden crucifix and candle-sticks caught the light where they stood on the embroidered white altar cloth.

Our decision to marry that day had been made quickly, and so only a few people attended. Even my daughters could not make arrangements to get away in time, and the only guests on the bride's side of the church were four Benedictine nuns from a monastery in Windsor where I had done some volunteer work. Bill's sister was my matron of honor, and Bill's father gave me away. His sons served as best men.

When I had chosen my dress and flowers, I had smiled to myself, knowing my mother would have loved my choice. I walked down the aisle in a blue velvet dress carrying one red rose.

The Episcopal priest who married us was a woman, a fact that filled me with joy. I felt the streams of my life flowing together into a single current. The cantor sang hymns I knew from grade school, and my four happy nuns received the Body of Christ with us in an Episcopal Church. The wedding ceremony itself was simple and lovely.

I was startled to see tears streaming down the groom's face, however. "Second thoughts?" I whispered to him.

He shook his head. "Tears of gratitude." My man was free enough to show his vulnerability in public, a memory I shall forever cherish.

During the ceremony, my eyes were fixed on the golden crucifix where it stood on the altar. For the first time in my life, I felt comfortable looking directly at Jesus. As a child, he had made me uncomfortable, because I knew I could never be his "one-and-only." Now that I had found someone who loved me in that way—I knew I was truly Bill's one-and-only—I was struck with a sudden realization: each and every one of us is Jesus' one-and-only. He loves us each uniquely.

I gave a sigh, as though I had finally come home after a long and weary journey. I knew my life now would be inextricably connected to Jesus, for He had given me Bill.

19

Look!
I'm doing something new.
It's sprouting right now.
Do you see it?
I will even make a path for you
straight through uncharted territory.
Isaiah 43:19

The romance was wonderful—but moving to upstate New York was not easy. New York City was in my blood, and upstate, however beautiful, seemed strange and foreign. I missed the theaters, the restaurants, and the museums. I missed the humor; when I made a joke here, no one seemed to get it. Most of all, I missed the city's incredible energy. More than ever, I missed my three daughters who were three thousand miles away.

I told myself it takes time to acclimate. In the meantime, I began looking for a ministry. I contacted every nearby church—and then one day I knocked on the door of St. Anthony of Padua in Endicott, New York. A white-haired nun with a young face answered the door.

"Hello," I said. "I'm new to the area—and I'm looking for some sort of ministry."

She immediately invited me in, and after reading my résumé, she said, "How would you like to write a spiritual column for our parish newsletter?"

And so my ministry at St. Anthony of Padua began. In time, I asked the pastor if I could start a spiritual reading group. He liked the idea, and eight women joined. The women were seeking answers, and they were satisfied with nothing less than truth.

I also spoke at women's retreats. After one of these, the pastor asked if he could talk with me. "I heard you speak the other night," he said, "and I had an idea."

I looked at him, waiting for whatever would come next.

"I'm afraid homilies bore most people," he said. "Not that people should come to Mass for entertainment, of course. But I wondered—maybe every couple of months we could offer them something different. A skit. I thought maybe you'd be able to write the script and then direct it. Maybe even act in it. Maybe you could bring the Gospel alive in a new way." He held out his hands and shrugged. "I'd like to give it a try. What do you think?"

I couldn't contain my excitement and joy. "What do I think?" I screamed. "I think it's a fantastic idea! When do we begin?"

Finally, I was doing what I had always loved most. The skits expanded beyond Mass and were incorporated into retreats. As I wrote and acted, I felt the Gospel characters come alive—for me, as well as the congregation.

St. Anthony's Italian-American congregation opened their arms to me. I was humbled by their acceptance of me, a laywoman who had come out of nowhere, who preached to them from the pulpit and did things in church they had never seen before.

And then one day I used a Sufi prayer or two during retreats. People told me the beauty of the words resonated in their hearts. Once again, the people of St. Anthony's took me by surprise with their willingness to open themselves to new ideas outside traditional Catholicism. In the retreats I led now, the Sufi and Christian paths complemented each other, as I was convinced they were meant to do. All the parts of me were coming together as well.

And most of all, my voice was being heard.

I was amazed and grateful for the magnanimity of God's providence. I had given up my life to marry Bill— only to find it again in a new way.

And God had still more surprises in store me.

✳✳✳

One Easter I decided to make a Holy Week retreat offered by the Sisters of the Cenacle in Westchester County, New York. I kissed Bill good-bye and headed off happily for some spiritual nourishment.

After dinner on Holy Thursday evening, one of the sisters called me over to the television set. I was surprised the nuns would consider watching television an appropriate activity for Holy Week, but the nun laughed at my expression and said, "It's all right. It's Father Thomas Keating. Have you heard of him?"

I nodded. "His name is familiar, but I really don't know who he is."

"Well, sit down and listen. He's about to be interviewed."

So I sat and listened as Father Keating spoke of a method of prayer he called centering prayer. I felt a stirring inside me, a sense that I was hearing something I deeply needed. I thought back to the longings for stillness I had experienced when I was first living on my own after the Abode. Was this the answer to my yearning?

I asked the sister if she would teach me Father Keating's method of prayer during the retreat.

"Well, first you choose a sacred word," she told me at our first session together. "It could be 'Jesus' or 'Abba' or simply 'love.' It's anything that will be symbol of your willingness to be open to God's presence within you. But it's not a mantra, the way Eastern religions use them, not something to be repeated over and over. You use the word only when you realize that you have a thought—or a feeling or any sensation at all, like your nose itching. Are you with me so far?"

I stifled a giggle and nodded.

"So what's left?" She thought for a moment, and then answered her own question: "Plenty, but the basics are simple. You get comfortable, close your eyes, and breathe deeply. The moment you become aware of a thought—or feeling or sensation—you turn back to the sacred word and say it silently. Then you let it go and go on centering yourself in God's presence."

For the remainder of the retreat, I attempted to practice this method of prayer. I experienced nothing that seemed spiritual in the least, only frustration! I couldn't rid myself of thoughts no matter how hard I tried.

This was perfectly normal and only to be expected, but I didn't know it then. I went home feeling as though I had failed to grasp this new form of prayer. But I knew even then that centering prayer was something I would come back to.

✳✳✳

Meanwhile, after seven years at St. Anthony's, I began to sense that it was time for me to move on. I loved the people and my work, but somehow I also knew I had to leave if I wanted to keep growing.

"Grow?" asked that familiar sarcastic voice inside my head. "As what? Into what?" I hadn't the slightest idea. I only knew I needed to be free to learn more about God and the spiritual realms. This time I knew enough not to seek out a university or some other academic avenue. Instead, I was convinced I needed to go into my own self to find the answers. Feeling both heartsick and hopeful, I wrote my letter of resignation to St. Anthony's pastor.

20

You sit there day after day, saying to yourself,
"This is a strange business."
You're the strange business!
You have the sun's energy within you,
but you keep it knotted up at the base of your spine.
You're some crazy kind of gold
that wants to remain inside the furnace,
so you won't have to be shaped into coins.
Rumi

I had taken a leap of faith when I left St. Anthony's—and plunged deep into yet another dark-night-of-the-soul experience.

By this time Bill and I had moved to Pennsylvania, only minutes from the New York border, where Bill had built a house on a lake. The place is beautiful and serene. You'd think it would be a veritable haven for someone who wanted to write, to pray, to simply be.

Instead, I felt isolated there, especially when winter fell. The endless snow created a colorless, desolate world. I felt abandoned, lonely.

Each morning I would wake up and look out the window at yet another gray day. "I hate living here!" I finally burst out. "I never see people, and everything is drab. Even the light looks different here from what it does in the city. There's *less* of it."

Bill looked at me as though I had lost my mind. But I couldn't stop now. "And the snow," I sputtered. "The endless snow! I hate it! Everything is white! I'm surrounded in white—white, white, white!"

"But it's beautiful," Bill protested. "It makes me feel cozy inside, while everything outside is cold. And the snow is lovely . . . ethereal."

"Ethereal my foot!" I threw up my hands in frustration. "Oh, you're no help. I'm imprisoned, surrounded by *white*. And it's always so damned cold."

"I'll turn the heat up."

I sighed. "I don't want you to turn up the heat. I don't want you to do anything except to move to California with me—where there's sunshine and warmth. And people are as nuts as I am! I don't *fit* here."

I knew we couldn't move to California. Bill had spent his life's savings building the house. He loved every bit of living there: the house, the lake, the land, the white world that surrounded us all winter long. And he didn't like California.

But I resented him for loving the place I hated. And I resented my daughters for living three thousand miles away, where I couldn't be a part of their lives and my grandchildren's lives.

Gradually, I became aware that all my resentment and my hatred of the place was masking something deeper, something that twisted my physical innards until they felt like wrung-out rags. I couldn't get a handle on what I was experiencing. I couldn't see what it *meant*. I remembered the winter days when I was a teenager and played hooky from school—but there was nowhere for me to escape to here in the wilds of Pennsylvania. I felt like a caged animal.

And God? Where had He gone to? After all I had experienced, the long journey that had led me to this place, how could I no longer feel His presence? Finally, what pushed into my consciousness was the horrendous fear that this God whom I thought I had found was only an illusion, an imaginary friend I had made up for my own comfort. And if this were so, then everything I had believed, taught, preached, endured—all of it—were lies. It was all a delusion.

What is truth? Pilate asked the same question long ago. As far as I know, he never got an answer. How could I recognize truth? And why does such never-ending pain go along with the search for truth? I knew the pain was no guarantee that truth would ever be found. It was just pain, walking beside me, goading me, tempting me to give up on life rather than endure the endless questions.

Regardless of where I turned, I was thrown back upon myself. I had left St. Anthony's so I could devote myself to an inner journey, but I had found only darkness inside myself, a darkness that matched the winter world around me. I had no energy for spiritual reading or attending liturgy or caring for myself. All I wanted was to rid myself of the pain by going to sleep. I knew these were the symptoms of clinical depression; I may have been experiencing a form of seasonal affective disorder. But that was no comfort.

Was life no more than a huge cosmic joke? I couldn't rid my thought of the existential horror that ultimately there is nothing at all. Everything I had "accomplished" I now saw as emptiness. My voice was silenced again; my very identity seemed to have faded into the endless white days. The only thing left was a terrible, relentless fear that wrapped its tentacles around my mind.

I continued to attempt to pray, but it seemed like an empty, useless practice. I had no choice but to surrender to the fear and allow it to take me wherever it wanted. Then one day while I was yet again going through the motions of prayer, I felt what seemed like a physical pain at the base of my spine. I tried to ignore it, but it shifted, moving up and down my vertebrae. I breathed into the pain, thinking that would help me cope with it. As I breathed, suddenly the pain was transformed into something that "felt" and "looked" like a Communion Host.

As usual, whenever I've had one of these odd experiences, I doubted myself. I discounted it as my imagination, a product of my yearning for meaning, for God's presence. But it was an odd thing, that sensation of a small, perfect white circle within my very bones.

I found myself remembering that Jesus had said, "By their fruits you will know. . . ." I decided I would wait to see what the fruits of this experience were. In the meantime, I knew enough to detach myself from it and let it go.

A sense of love began to wrap around me, despite the endless snow. And then the long, hard, winter finally ended. Spring came. It brought with it a new phase of my spiritual life.

I discovered that Father Keating's organization, Contemplative Outreach, was offering a correspondence course in the history and practice of centering prayer. I decided to take the course.

My mentor was a sister of Notre Dame de Namur, Sister Maryanne Laughlin, who lived in Manchester, New Hampshire. We spoke on the phone once a week; in between our conversations, I immersed myself in the course.

When the course was finished, Sister Maryanne asked me if I'd like to visit her retreat house in Manchester. I was delighted at the prospect. Once again, I said good-bye to Bill and drove off on a spiritual adventure.

21

In prayer, I feel my spirit and soul rise effortlessly,
suspended above this life,
fixed in God, centered and at rest. . . .
That which normally supports the self disappears;
that which she once depended on
would now only hold her back.

Brother Lawrence of the Resurrection

Maryanne was standing at the door waiting for me when
I arrived. She was a woman in her late sixties, tall, a bit
plump, and not attractive if measured by Hollywood's
standards. But she had a smile to die for! She held out her
arms and pulled me against her. "You must be exhausted.
Come, let me take your bags."

We climbed two flights of stairs. On the top floor, she
put down the bags and said, "Well, take your pick. White,
purple, yellow, or pink." Each of the four rooms had a
double bed with a pile of lacy pillows that matched the
white, purple, yellow, or pink bedspread. Lace curtains
hung to the floor from the windows, while a comfortable
chair, a desk, and a small table were arranged to make

each room feel cozy and welcoming. A pretty sign fancily inscribed with the name of a saint was on each door.

"So," Maryanne said, "do you like it?"

"Like it? I can hardly believe it. It's so unlike any retreat house I've ever known." I didn't dare mention to her the Sufi retreats I had attended!

"Well, I believe a person on retreat should feel comfortable and happy if she is to make a good retreat. After all, our Lord is full of bounty. So tonight I'm taking you out to dinner."

"What?" I was truly confused now. "I don't understand."

She laughed. "What's there to understand? You must begin your retreat with joy, so I'm taking you out to dinner. Okay?"

"Okay." I wasn't sure what to think.

Maryanne gave me another hug. "Now, you unpack and rest with the Lord. When it's time to leave for dinner, I'll call you."

I chose Sister Julie Billiart's room, the purple room. Sister Julie was the founder of Maryanne's order, the Sisters of Notre Dame de Namur. Aside from founding the order and her charitable works, I knew that Sister Julie had been famous for her smile; she was often referred to as the "happy nun." Sister Maryanne seemed to me to be a lot like the founder of her order.

I sat down on the bed and looked around the comfortable room. I noticed an empty niche in the wall opposite the bed, and I wondered why it had been included in the room's design. My attention turned next to the end table beside the bed, where a small sign read, "Stay in your cell, and your cell will tell you everything." I knew it was a saying from one of the fourth-century Desert Fathers. As I looked next at the lacy lilac rocker chair that stood beside the window, I doubted the Desert Fathers' cells had been much like this one!

Maryanne and I dined at a restaurant overlooking the water. She ordered for both of us: pork loin, roasted potatoes and carrots, salad, and for dessert, blueberry pie with vanilla ice cream. Oh yes, and wine.

When we returned to the retreat house, she lingered in my bedroom doorway. "You know what to expect from this retreat, right? This is a centering prayer retreat."

I laughed. "I know it's centering prayer—but I don't have a clue what to expect!"

Maryanne laughed too. "The Holy Spirit will take it from here. But be prepared—during centering prayer, stuff tends to rise from the unconscious. It's one of the prayer's goodies! All the junk you've stuck out of sight— maybe even for a lifetime—suddenly floats to the surface. It may hurt—but it will leave you freer. More open to God."

I looked at her doubtfully. "Isn't that . . . difficult?"

Maryanne nodded, smiling happily. "Oh, yes, many a tear has fallen during centering prayer. And much joy springs to the surface as well. Either way, the goal of the prayer is only one thing—union with God." She looked at my expression and winked. "Don't worry! The Holy Spirit is in charge."

She turned to go, then paused and said over her shoulder, "Would you like to have the Blessed Sacrament in your room?"

I nearly choked. "What? Is that—possible?"

"Oh, yes," she said. "I cleared it with the pastor. I'll bring it right up."

Minutes later, the Eucharist was resting in the small niche I had noticed in the wall. Maryanne lit a candle that would burn as long as the Host was there, knelt before it for a moment, and then left me.

I sat on my bed and looked at the Eucharist. After growing up Catholic, I still believe that the Host—the small white wafer, like the one I had felt within my spine—fully contains the body and blood of Christ, a full and real expression of Christ on earth. And now I had Christ in the room with me.

The intimacy of having him there with me overwhelmed me with joy. But at the same time, I felt a little awkward. I didn't know quite what to do or how to behave. Should I undress in the bathroom? Should I genuflect each time I passed the tabernacle? I'd be genuflecting all night!

Before I could settle on answers to these questions, I fell asleep, exhausted after my long day.

When I woke, there was the Blessed Sacrament waiting quietly for me in its little niche, the candle flame still glowing. I sat up in bed and prayed for a few moments, then decided to get up and go to Mass.

Maryanne was already there. I discovered she attended daily Mass and also spent an hour in the

Adoration chapel early each morning at three. Despite this discipline of prayer, she also ran the retreat house singlehandedly.

Later that morning, breakfast was served in silence on a table that held both flowers and food, with bright napkins that matched the tablecloth. The word "ascetic" was simply not part of Maryanne's vocabulary.

After the delicious meal, I asked Maryanne how much I should pay her for the retreat.

She shook her head. "I never charge money for my retreats."

I looked around the place. I thought about all the food I had just eaten. "Maryanne, how can you keep this house running without money?"

She shrugged. "Well, it's been running for twenty years now, so I guess I'll just keep doing what I'm doing. Besides, the Holy Spirit is in charge, not me. Leave a love offering if you want. Or don't." She laughed. "God is bountiful. He'll take care of this place."

As I helped her clear the table, I decided the woman had to run on some sort of Spirit energy. She seemed constantly charged with an endless, tireless joy.

***

In the days that followed, I dove deeper into centering prayer. I learned it was a form of silent prayer intended to allow us to experience God's presence directly, closer than our own breath, closer than our thoughts, closer even than our very consciousness.

"It's both a relationship with God," Maryanne told me, "and a discipline that creates a place for that relationship to grow."

She left me alone in my room for long periods, so that I could practice, but she also talked with me. "Don't make the mistake of thinking centering prayer will replace all the other kinds of prayer," she told me. "It doesn't. But it adds more depth, more meaning to the other prayer. Those prayers are more like conversations with God. Centering prayer is communion with God. It will become the background, the ocean, you might say, on which all your other prayers float."

It wasn't easy. I'd sit myself down, close my eyes, and instead of peace, I found nothing but thoughts going round and round in my head, like a carousel that had come off its mooring. I'd immediately return to my sacred word; after about ten minutes, things would begin to calm down. The carousel's movement would become less frenetic, so that I could take a step back from it, let it drift from my awareness. In those moments, I floated in the Presence of God. Sometimes, I had no memory of what I experienced during those long, quiet hours in my room. I only knew that I was left with a deep well of joy inside me.

On the second or third day of the retreat, as I sat in my room by the Blessed Sacrament, I became aware of something inside me, a feeling of such love and sweetness that I didn't dare move. The sensation was a physical feeling; I felt it in my solar plexus, and yet at the same time, it flowed like electricity through my entire body.

I sat still, hardly breathing, as though I were in the presence of some shy, wild animal that might flee if I startled it. I heard myself say, "I love you."

And then, somewhere in the distance, Maryanne's voice called me to lunch. The moment was gone.

✳✳✳

After that, centering prayer seemed easier. It was best in the mornings, I found, when my head wasn't yet filled with worries and frustrations. But despite the sense of love and joy I was feeling, I doubted myself, as I have always done. What if I were doing the prayer incorrectly? What if I were just kidding myself that I was experiencing something wonderful? What if I had gotten some vital point all wrong?

When I confessed my fears to Maryanne, she shook her head. "That's the one thing you must never worry about—doing it wrong! You can't do this prayer wrong. There is no right or wrong. If your desire is for a deeper relationship with Christ, then that's all that matters. You can just rest in that desire. Emotions come and go. Thoughts come and go." She looked at my face, and then she sighed. "People always think they can do this wrong. But here's what Father Keating said: 'You can't do it wrong, unless you get up and walk away!' Got it? Are we clear now?"

"Yes, ma'am," I said meekly.

"Good! Now I have more important things to do." She gave me a wink. "I need to make up my mind whether to have raspberry cheesecake or chocolate mousse for dessert before it gets too late." She flapped her hand at me. "Go and enjoy God. Have fun, and stop worrying over nothing!"

And so I went back to my room. By the afternoon, I needed exercise, so I walked through the city, trying hard not to let myself be distracted by the noises of traffic, people talking on the sidewalks, children playing. Somehow, the walk helped me integrate the retreat silence with my own noisy heart.

When I got back, it was time for me to meet with Maryanne for spiritual direction. Afterward, I asked her if Father Keating had ever visited this retreat house. The more time I spent with his method of prayer, the more curious I felt about the man.

"Not yet," Maryanne replied, "but I plan to get him over here one of these days. You know he was the abbot of St. Joseph's Monastery, which is only an hour and a half away from here?"

I shook my head. "I thought he was from New York."

"Yes, he grew up there." She sat back at her chair and looked at me. "Do you want me to tell you about him?"

I nodded, and Maryanne launched into Father Keating's story. I learned that his mother had been an Episcopalian and his father was a non-practicing Catholic—but he had an Irish Catholic nurse who made sure he went to Mass at the nearest Catholic church, a couple of miles from his home. When the woman who took care of the rectory told the pastor about the boy who was walking two miles to get to Mass, the pastor wanted to talk to him. Eventually, Thomas and the priest formed a close bond.

When World War II began, Thomas was going to enlist, but the pastor told him that the war was not for him. Thomas obeyed the priest's advice, but he felt guilty about not serving with his friends in the military. After a long period of discernment, though, he decided to become a Trappist monk and was sent to a monastery somewhere in Rhode Island. One night a terrible fire hit the monastery, and it burned to the ground. Nothing was left, and so the monks decided to move to Massachusetts, where together, all by themselves, they built a new monastery they named St. Joseph's. Thomas would be the abbot at this monastery for twenty years.

In the 1960s, hippies came knocking at the monastery door, inquiring about the nearest Buddhist monastery. They wanted to learn how to meditate. Their questions made Thomas curious, and he decided to look into his own tradition to see if he could find something similar. What he found was that Christianity has a rich tradition of contemplative prayer among the saints and mystics—but the Church had never encouraged this form of prayer. Thomas felt the time was ripe to move contemplative prayer into Christianity's mainstream. With two priests from the Abbey, William Menninger and Basil

Pennington, he put together a method of contemplation that became known as centering prayer.

"Now," finished Maryanne, "there are centering prayer retreats and workshops and centers all over the world, all thanks to Father Keating. I tell you, the man is a living saint. So, yes, I'm going to get him to come here no matter what it takes!"

✳✳✳

That evening, back in my room, I thought about what Maryanne had said, and I remembered the days when I first moved to Douglaston and had tried so hard to imitate the life of Teresa of Avila. I remembered also my readings in John of the Cross: "Silence," wrote John, "is the voice of God."

And now, with a sense of homecoming, I recognized that this prayer was similar to what I had learned as a Sufi. On those long Sufi retreats, each of the practices I was given began with a particular sound or word—a wazifa—but they always ended in silence. Like Father Keating's sacred word, we used the sound or word only as a tool, a means of entry into the Beloved's deep silence—and then we let it go. In the days when I sometimes did zikr a thousand times a day, I would be transported into a silent space where time and place vanished, leaving the emptiness of the Divine Presence. During those times, I was aware of myself, but I was also beyond myself: beyond all joy or despair, beyond consciousness itself—and yet fully conscious and fully alive. My voicelessness dropped away into the silence. In the silence, it no longer mattered.

I never wanted those moments to end—and yet I left them behind when I left the Sufis. I realized now that my yearning for that silent paradise had brought me here, to this place, to Father Keating's centering prayer, to Maryanne. If I were not a Sufi, I would not be rediscovering Christianity.

With this realization, I could finally open myself to centering prayer and truly grasp what it was all about. I remembered that the great Sufi poet Rumi had described the same state of consciousness that centering prayer brings:

> There's nothing left of me.
> I'm like a ruby held up to the sunrise.
> Is it still a stone,
> or a world made of redness?
> It has no resistance to sunlight.
> The ruby and the sunrise are one.

Flowing out from these moments of prayer, I began to notice a tendency to slow down, to be more aware of the moment, to listen for the silent call of my name. This call lay waiting just beneath the surface of life, I realized, moment by moment, if I was only aware. Whenever I was distracted, though, no longer truly present, I missed hearing that still, small voice. I soon learned that the buzz of negative thoughts—judgment, anger, alienation, fear—interfered more than anything else with my perception of the silence that called to me.

I also learned I could do nothing to *make* the silence speak. Finally, I truly grasped that I could not do this wrong! My old fears about my own incompetence dropped away, irrelevant. I sat in silence and waited to see what would happen next.

In the same poem, Rumi continued:

> *Submit to a daily practice.*
> *Your loyalty to that is a ring on the door.*
> *Keep knocking, and the joy inside*
> *will eventually open a window*
> *and look out to see who's there.*

When the retreat was nearly over, Maryanne asked me, "How'd you like to come visit my Beloved, the Fourth?"

"Who?"

"My Beloved. Father Robert. He's a Trappist monk at St. Joseph's Abbey in Massachusetts, about an hour and a half away. You should see the Abbey anyway. It'll be good for you."

And off we went. She sped over the hills—her driving style was more akin to flying—with me saying a prayer I'd live to see Bill again. To distract myself from my white-knuckled grip on the armrest, I asked her, "Why do you call him your Beloved, the Fourth?"

She turned to me and grinned. "Because he's so dear to me."

I wished she wouldn't take her eyes off the road when she talked to me, but I asked her anyway, "How did you meet him?"

This time, to my relief, she kept her eyes on the road ahead as she answered. "Before I began the retreat house, I had left the motherhouse, not knowing what turn my life would take next. Father Robert was my spiritual director. He suggested I make a long retreat—it lasted almost a year—and that I'd know at the end of the retreat what I could do next. That's how the retreat house was born. He was my retreat master during that time, and his guidance saved me from a problem I'd had all my life."

She fell silent. I waited, hoping she would continue but not wanting to pry. After a moment, she said, "I was haunted with guilt all my life. 'Scrupulosity' is the old-fashioned word we use in orders. In psychiatric terms, it was an obsessive thought pattern, always present. I couldn't shake it."

I looked at the smiling woman beside me; I had never known anyone who exuded a sense of constant peace and well-being as much as she did. It was hard to imagine her plagued with guilt.

She glanced at me again and laughed at my expression. "I know, I know, it's hard to believe seeing me now. But it was so bad that Father Robert said I needed therapy—and then he got permission to attend each session with me." She gave her head a little nod. "So that's why I call him my Beloved. I wouldn't be who I am today without him."

"But what's 'the Fourth' all about?"

"Oh," she said with a perfectly straight face, "the Fourth Person of the Blessed Trinity, of course."

***

The Abbey was on a hill, surrounded by rolling hills that looked like the soft folds of a child's blanket. We parked the car and followed a cloister walk to the church. I felt as though I had stepped inside a hidden world. Lilacs and lilies, roses and forget-me-nots bloomed everywhere.

Inside the church, I looked up at the stained-glass window behind the main altar: a large-eyed Mary held on her lap Jesus as a small boy. He, in turn, held the blue globe of the world. A crimson halo surrounded Mary's head, and her feet rested on the moon's gold sickle. Smaller windows of deep blue and bright gold framed the central window, casting a sense of deep, bright mystery across the church's interior.

At last, I looked away from Mary's gentle face. A simple cross hung above me from the ceiling. In front of the altar, wooden rows faced each other where the monks sat for daily prayers and Mass; deeper in the nave, straight-backed pews were reserved for the public. When I turned back toward the door through which we'd entered, I saw a blue and crimson rose window glowing in the peak of the nave. The entire space seemed filled with the palpable presence of Christ.

We went back to the car and drove around the church to the field beyond. In the distance, Father Robert was shepherding sheep and a llama into the barn. We walked across the field, and Maryanne introduced me. Then she turned to me and grinned. "Well, here he is, the Fourth."

He shrugged, as though the name embarrassed him. He was a tall man, kind and gentle, with a sweet smile. I learned later he had been in the Abbey since he was twenty-one. He told me, "I just always knew this was what I wanted. And I wanted the hardest path I could find. At the time I entered, way before Vatican II, the Trappist rule was the strictest and the most difficult, so I chose it. A lot of machismo was involved. But this place soon tore that out of me."

Robert led us on a tour around the monastery and the grounds. I learned that the monks themselves had built the stone buildings. Earlier in their history, they had grown their own fruits and vegetables and made their own wine, but when their numbers decreased, they switched to making an assortment of things for sale: jellies, jams, cakes, beer, and wooden carvings. Directing retreats, writing books, and operating a bookstore also helped them survive.

Maryanne had brought along a picnic lunch of shrimp, biscuits, and potato salad. I could tell she was in her glory, doting on Robert like a mother hen. I could also see that these two people loved each other very much.

In the years since I've known them both, I've realized that everyone knows about their love—the abbot at St. Joseph's, Robert's fellow monks, and Maryanne's friends and acquaintances. Robert and Maryanne make no effort to conceal their love. Its purity far outweighs any threat of scandal.

As I watched them together on that first day when I met Father Robert, I found myself remembering something the Sufis used to say: When we search for love we are really searching for God. When we find someone to love, that person's soul somehow resonates with ours, but it goes even deeper, for it is God in us loving God in the other. This was what I sensed flowing back and forth between Maryanne and Robert, a pure, shining example of Divine love.

I thought of a famous *hadith* (one of the sayings traditionally attributed to the Prophet Muhammad) that the Sufis loved:

> *When I love him, I become his ears, his eyes, his tongue, his hands, his legs and his heart: he hears by Me, he speaks by Me, he handles by Me, he walks by Me and he comprehends by Me.*

It's what Christ meant when he said, "The Father and I are one"; what Saint Paul meant when he said, "I no longer live, not I, but Christ lives in me." It is the essence of *oneness*, expressed in human relationships—and it is all God.

We drove back to the retreat house silently. My head was too full of new thoughts and realizations for me to talk.

✳✳✳

Saying good-bye to Maryanne at the end of the ten-day retreat wasn't easy. I knew I would see this wonderful woman again, but in the meantime, I'd miss her spontaneity and laughter, her magnanimity and her unbridled trust in God's providence.

But I went home a happy woman, happy to see Bill, happy with the memories of Robert and Maryanne, and most of all, happy with my new understanding of centering prayer.

I was faithful to centering prayer. Its twice-a-day discipline became a part of my days' structure. The bright summer days slid by, and I enjoyed my home on the lake.

And then summer changed to fall, and fall to winter. The cold, dark days came again, as they always do. Once again, winter clouded everything I thought and did, and I felt like a caged animal in the quiet, isolated house. I wanted to escape the confines of home . . . of marriage . . . of life itself. I resented Bill's constant enjoyment of the place; I longed to see my kids; I yearned to see more people. I felt silenced, smothered, invisible. I wanted to be heard, to breathe, to be seen. I wanted *out*.

But out of what? I didn't know. I'd go around in circles like this for days at a time. What was worst to bear was my sense of failure. I had thought with centering prayer, winter's darkness would not get to me the way it had before. And yet here I was again, right back where I'd been the year before, as though nothing had happened between now and then, as though I'd learned nothing from Maryanne.

At first I told myself I was simply suffering from seasonal affective disorder, so I bought a sun lamp. It didn't help. I tried psychological therapy and antidepressants. They helped, but only on a superficial level. Centering prayer was my only source of relief. But it was not the cure I had hoped it would be.

Then, as I re-read John of the Cross and his description of the soul's dark nights, I made a connection to another Sufi concept: *qabd* (contraction) and *bast* (openness). Qabd means being caught, distressed, grasped tight as though you were inside a fist. The Sufis used the word to describe those times when a person feels as though her link with the source of her spiritual light has been severed, causing pain and a sense of spiritual blockage. Bast, on the other hand, describes openness, expansion, relief, and freedom. When a person is experiencing bast, the Sufis said, she is developing spiritually to the point that she becomes a vehicle of the Beloved, embracing all existence. The Sufis taught that both states were natural parts of the spiritual life.

"The heart is between the two Fingers of the All-Merciful," is another saying attributed to the Prophet. "To remind us of this fact, He turns it from state to state and gives it whatever form He wishes."

Rumi wrote:

Observe the expansion
and contraction of your hand:
you always open your fist after you close it.
If your fingers were always closed
or always opened,
you would be crippled.
Your life's movement
is also governed by these two qualities:
expansion and contraction.
They are both as necessary to you
as a bird's two wings.

Each state has gifts to give. Expansion brings joy, delight, new discoveries—while contraction humbles us, fills us with yearning for a deeper understanding of the Divine.

As I read John of the Cross, I recognized the same ideas. My feelings of despair and frustration didn't go away, but I began to glimpse that the darkness might have a meaning far deeper than my awareness. John wrote:

One dark night,
fired with love's urgent longing
—oh, the sheer grace!—
I went out, unseen by anyone,
leaving my silent house.

John of the Cross found in his darkness the yearning passion of a frustrated lover. He accepted his quiet, empty house, his sense of invisibility, seeing both not as a trap but as an opportunity to slip away and go into a deeper, more intimate relationship with God.

All that, of course, is an attempt to make sense of an experience that remains fathomless. Even today, I continue to have these bouts of darkness. I would like to say that I endure them with better grace than I once did; that I understand better their proper relationship to winter, my marriage, my domicile, my spiritual life; and that I have achieved a modicum of control over them.

Fat chance!

Recently, I've accepted that perhaps I will never name and understand these times. Maybe I'll know what's been going on after my death, in the presence of eternity. Perhaps I'm not supposed to know. Whatever it is that I experience each winter, it is contained in the mystery of God. The question then becomes: Can I surrender to mystery? To not knowing? Can I be content to dwell for a time in the constriction of dark nights?

I'm afraid I can't. Not now. Not yet. My pride is too strong and my thirst for truth too overwhelming. And yet, perhaps, that is exactly the point. In the helplessness and frustration of not knowing, I touch something deeper and more real than I can ever reach in the moments when I feel clear and strong. To use Rumi's metaphor, without the dark, constricted days, I would be like a one-winged bird, unable to truly fly.

In any event, the seasons change, and dark nights always fade away into months of light. Life continued. Bill and I fought and made up, laughed and loved each other. My daughters seemed happy in their lives in California and Oregon; I had six beautiful grandchildren; and except for an occasional battle with Crohn's disease, all was going well in my life. The years' circle of months turned around and around.

And then the stability of that cycle was shattered. Bill needed open heart surgery.

22

These pains you feel are messengers.
Listen to them.
Rumi

He survived the surgery. He recovered. He even insisted on acting as though he'd never had a thing wrong with his heart and went back to doing all the things he'd always done, swimming and kayaking on the lake in the summer, skating in winter. But I couldn't recover as quickly. The fear of losing him had been too great.

And then, a year later, he was diagnosed with an aggressive prostrate cancer. Everything happened very quickly, and life was suddenly out of control. I was help-less. The future loomed like a dark wall, enclosing me in what seemed like a vast desert. What was the point of it all, all the beauty of life, if it could disappear so suddenly?

As I tried to pray, tried to surrender Bill's life into the Divine hand, I had a sudden memory: when I was in Egypt, one day we rode camels across the sands of the Sahara Desert. From my lofty, rocking seat, I saw in the midst of the barren world a white cactus flower whose crimson center brimmed like blood. All alone, it seemed to nestle into the fierce heat and desolate land, its beauty serene, unconcerned. It made me think of the man from Nazareth, his vulnerability to the world's hatred and violence, his conscious acceptance of death and loss.

I found myself resonating with the pain of Christ, as though my smaller pain thrummed with a deep, cosmic vibration. I'm convinced now that when we suffer tragedy in whatever form—the loss of a loved one, terminal illness, horrendous accidents—we participate in the suffering of the Mystical Body of Christ. We are, in some inexplicable way, helping Jesus carry his cross as he helps us carry ours. The crucifixion is not restricted to that one time two thousand years ago. God did not step on the Earth in a brief moment and then hop out again. He remains inside us, outside us, with us. He suffers when we suffer, is comforted when we're comforted.

Moreover, in some inscrutable way, when we participate in the suffering of Christ, we also tap into the universe. The world vibrates with pain. We would like to ignore it. We would prefer to hold ourselves separate from it. But in suffering, as we open our soul—like a white-petaled flower—we become united with a vast, timeless community.

And then, beneath the tears and the anguish, in the midst of the desert's fierce heat, we find that glowing crimson secret, like a blood-red jewel hidden in the darkness.

Poetry and theology weren't much help, of course, in the moments when I was simply and utterly terrified that I was going to lose my husband. During this time, it was Father Robert who helped me most. He listened to my jumble of thoughts and emotions, and then, as though he were piecing together a complicated puzzle, he calmly and gently made sense of it all for me. He told me that when he first entered the monastery, Father Thomas Keating, who was then Abbot of St. Joseph's, had helped him immensely by simply naming each of these painful experiences as yet another "dark night," something natural and to be expected, something that would inevitably come to an end, leaving behind spiritual gifts.

In the eighteenth-century, Father Robert reminded me, the Jesuit priest named Jean-Pierre de Caussade had written his little book, *Abandonment to Divine Providence*. "Here's what we need to remember from de Caussade, Marietta," Robert told me. "'What God arranges for us to experience at each moment is the best and holiest thing that could happen to us.'"

Then, just as I was feeling a moment of lofty spirituality, Robert gave me his sweet smile and said, "Cheer up. It can only get worse!"

I couldn't help but snicker—but I also wanted to give this lovely, spiritual man a good kick.

"Don't take yourself so seriously," he said. "All this, so much of life, is God playing."

I bridled at this. How could I help but take these things seriously? What was I supposed to do? Go out dancing? Some God, if this was the way He played!

I went home, and sought comfort and answers in my reading, as I always had. Again and again as I read, I came across the same thought Father Robert had offered me. Magdeburg, a mystic of the Middle Ages, wrote, "The soul is taken by God to a secret place . . . and God alone will play with it in a game of which the body knows nothing." In my Buddhist reading, I found the "laughter in the void"; "when you realize how perfect everything is," said the Buddha, "you will tilt back your head and laugh at the sky." I read a Hindu author who spoke of acknowledging the futility of life and our attachment to it by laughing and singing, dancing and playing with the Lord. Saint Augustine spoke of the game of "hide and seek" being played within him; "I am aware," he wrote, "of something in myself, like a light dancing before my soul . . . it hides and, then again, it shows." The fourteenth-century Dominican mystic, Meister Eckhart, exclaimed, "Do you know what goes on in the core of the Trinity? In the core of the Trinity, the Father laughs and gives birth to the Son, and the Son laughs back at the Father and gives birth to the Spirit and the whole Trinity laughs and gives birth to us!" The Dutch theologian Hans Urs von Balthasar wrote, "Divine play is a reflection of a wider reality, just as goodness, truth and beauty are reflections of the same."

My beloved Sufis knew all this as well, of course, but somehow I had failed to absorb the message. The fourteenth-century Sufi poet Hafiz spoke of a "playful God"; he wrote, "The Beloved sometimes wants to do us a great favor, so he holds us upside down and shakes all the nonsense out. When He is in such a playful, drunken mood, though, most everyone I know tries to run away!"

Modern Christianity has lost this sense of Divine playfulness. When we approach the Gospels with a strict literalism, we don't encounter a laughing Jesus, perhaps because his humor has slipped through the sieve of our far different culture and language. We don't get the joke, and we have focused instead on sadness and sin. But if you read between the lines, Christ's humor is still there. Peter alone would have given him cause to laugh!

I needed to awaken to a sense of play, I realized at last. For so long I had concentrated on the crucifixion, on the suffering and evil in the world. I had become so solemn about my spirituality; I took it very seriously; and I had forgotten Jesus' words: "Unless you become like little children, you cannot enter the kingdom of heaven." I had let life's horror, pain, and devastation blind me to the joy that lies within it, forever sustaining and young. Creation itself reveals a Divine sense of play, over and over again.

I wrote this prayer:

Play, my Beloved, play!
Swing on the trees adoring you.
Swim in the ocean reflecting you.
Gather the flowers mirroring your beauty

Play, my Beloved, play!
Dig deeply in the sand,
in the dark recesses of the earth.

Race with the flow of the wind,
glide on the caress of the air.

Play, my Beloved, play!
See your humor in a giraffe,
your happiness in a puppy,
your mischief in a kitten.

Play, my Beloved, play!
Grab us with your joy,
so that we ride a merry-go-round of ecstasy.
Hug us with your love,
and kiss us with your breath.

Play with us, Beloved, hide-and-seek,
so that what has been hidden
may now be revealed:
your play, Beloved, with that which is You.

As I opened myself to a sense of Divine playfulness and joy, the outer circumstances of my life began to change as well. To my intense relief and joy, Bill came through his ordeal and was soon on his way to full recovery. I no longer was swamped with terror and despair. But I still hadn't learned that the turning cycle of my emotional life tells me little about spiritual reality.

Emotions are tools we can use to perceive the spiritual world, just as our physical senses give us glimpses into the nature of reality—but all of them are limited. Our eyes and our fingers tell us that a table is a solid thing, but quantum physics says that the solid reality we perceive is just a trick of our senses; from the quantum perspective, nothing is solid, and the universe is a seething, swirling kettle of energy and potential. This doesn't mean we screw our eyes shut and wear mittens so that we'll never again be deceived by our senses of sight and touch—and we need not try to smother our emotions either. We do, however, need to recognize their limitations.

But I didn't know that yet—or I had forgotten it—when I pulled the Contemplative Outreach newsletter from my mail one day and read that Father Thomas Keating and two other presenters would be giving a twenty-one-day retreat. My heart leapt. I stuck the newsletter under Bill's nose and shouted, "Hey, what do you think? Should I go?"

He glanced at the paper, then smiled at me. "Sure, why not?"

23

What you seek
is seeking you.
Rumi

As I filled out the registration form, I plunged into a giddy sea of excitement. *Now, I'll get someplace,* I was thinking. *I'll go deeper and touch Divinity.* I floated on air through the remaining weeks until the retreat.

I just never learned.

I fell into long daydreams about the future: a position with Contemplative Outreach where my voice would be heard and respected . . . a personal relationship with Father Keating . . . travel around the world. The possibilities filled me with a heady joy.

Just as I was deceived during my dark nights into believing that reality was truly a dismal thing, now my emotions deceived me in a different way. Despite my constant hunger for spiritual truth, I continued to identify myself with the roles I played, instead of seeing that my identity—my true voice—was safely hidden elsewhere. I didn't know how to love myself without these roles to sustain my needy self-image. I so fiercely wanted to be identified as a spiritual being that I ignored my most sacred personhood as a unique expression of God. I failed to see that the desire to be seen as "spiritual" can be as ego-focused as any "worldly" goal.

In the Gospels, Jesus, like all wisdom teachers, uses strong language and exaggerated images to reveal the truth. "I have come to set a man against his father," he said, "and a daughter against her mother. Your enemies will be in your own house. You can't come to me without hating your father, mother, wife, child—even your own life" (Matt. 10:35, Luke 14:26). These abrasive phrases are meant to teach us that we cannot find our identities in people, nor in our ideas about who we are. We have to turn away from the false images. We are not who we think we are (any more than the seemingly solid table is what we think it is).

We are much more.

We need achieve nothing to prove our worth; we are already packaged in the "image and likeness of God." We are creatures of light, bearing within us (no matter how hidden) the spark of Divinity. But we are so easily hood-winked, so easily sidetracked from the truth.

The salvation Jesus offers us? I believe it's the chance to get back on the right track. To see ourselves—through no achievement of our own—as the embodiment of Divinity. To stop comparing ourselves to others, stop striving to prove our worth, and be free at last: free to be vehicles of Divine love.

When that happens, I suspect we might continue to be ambitious but not be driven; continue to work hard but not be compulsive; continue to dislike but not hate; and continue to love but not seek to possess. This is the detachment that Zen teaches. Rumi, the great Sufi mystic, put it this way: "Live in the nowhere that you come from, even though you have a local address."

After years of being on a spiritual path, I kept getting glimpses of these truths, but I still hadn't absorbed them. I was eager to teach others the wisdom I had gathered, but I was incapable of embodying what I taught.

The Sufis had taught me that every feeling—joy and sorrow, spitefulness and loving awareness—are merely unexpected guests to the home of our hearts—but I still clung to my ever-changing emotions as though they were solid reality.

Rumi wrote:

This human heart is a busy guesthouse.
Every morning there's a new arrival.
Happiness, sadness, irritation,
each fleeting feeling comes
as an unexpected visitor.
Welcome and entertain them all!
Even if a crowd of noisy sorrows
sweeps through your house,
knocking over all the furniture,
still, treat each guest with respect.

You never know.
Those violent, unpleasant guests
may actually be cleaning your house.
Now you'll have more room,
empty space available for a new delight.
So when dark thoughts,
even shame and malice,
come knocking
meet them at the door laughing.
Invite them in.
Be grateful for whatever comes
because each emotion is a guide
sent to you from a deeper world.

The Sufis used to say, "We work in the marketplace and sail the seven seas—but we always remember the God within. We struggle with the outer world, but inside we reside in our Paradise."

I sometimes think I forget more than I learn! The outer world distracts me; my thoughts elsewhere, I absentmindedly shove my life's most precious treasures under the sink like a bunch of dirty dishrags.

✳✳✳

When the day of the retreat finally arrived, I was a wreck. It was winter, snow-covered roads everywhere, and I had to drive to an unknown destination in Orange County, New York. To relieve my anxiety, Bill drove me.

He even got me there early. I kissed him good-bye, grateful for his love and support, and turned to face whatever lay ahead.

St. Andrews was a hundred-year-old retreat house run by the Sisters of Mercy. The building had once been a convent, and my room was a "cell," furnished only with a single bed, small desk, chair, and a lamp. I realized instantly that this wasn't going to be Sister Maryanne's idea of a retreat!

I unpacked my things and then wandered around, waiting for the others to get there. Once everyone had arrived, dinner was served early to allow us to talk and get acquainted. An hour later, a car pulled up in the driveway. We ran to the windows and saw two white-haired ladies emerge from the car with a tall, thin man. We all fell silent as we waited for him to come inside.

Father Keating's smile as he entered the room softened the intensity of his features. He shook hands with each of us and repeated each of our names, as though committing them to memory. I was intimidated, but his warmth and kindness put me at ease.

In the days that followed, I recognized another quality that flowed from him: a gentle and genuine humility. He never allowed anyone to serve him meals or get his morning coffee. He stopped for anyone who wished to speak with him, and he preferred to be called Thomas rather than Father Keating. After each time of centering prayer, he thanked us for being with him, as though we were the ones who had done him a favor. As the days went by, I was overwhelmed by his utter transparency. He was what he taught—and the focus of his teaching was love. As far as Thomas was concerned, all that exists, has existed, and will ever exist is surrounded and held in love.

Each morning of the retreat, we had an hour of centering prayer, and then after breakfast, Thomas gave a conference. A second hour of centering prayer came before lunch. Early afternoons were reserved for private sessions either with Thomas or another retreat guide. This was our time to pour out our individual heartaches, anxieties, and longings.

On a cold January afternoon, I had my first private session with Thomas. As I went to the appointment, I looked out the window at the winter world. Snowdrifts formed strange shapes outside the window, casting their cold, blue shadows across the white emptiness. And then I saw a cardinal, a splash of crimson feathers perched amid bare, dark branches. I drew in a deep breath and knocked on Father Keating's door.

The door opened, and I went in and took a seat facing him. I felt tongue-tied and shy, as though I were an awkward adolescent.

"What can I do for you today?" he asked.

"I'm not sure, really."

He smiled. "Well, start anywhere. You can talk to me about cooking if you wish. Just take your time."

"Okay." I managed a shaky smile. "But you'd be sorry if I talked about cooking!"

He smiled again and waited.

I sucked in another deep breath, trying to calm my nervousness. I knew I needed to talk to him about my recurring bouts of depression and emptiness, but I didn't know how to bring it up. I said instead, "I've been involved with Sufism for a number of years, and. . ." I couldn't think what else I wanted to say.

"Really?" His face lit with interest. "How wonderful for you. Which order were you associated with?"

"The Sufi Order of the West."

"Oh yes, that's the one in New Lebanon. Your spiritual leader there is Pir Vilayat."

I was astounded. "You're familiar with Pir Vilayat? With Sufism?"

"Yes, I've known your group in New Lebanon for a long time. What a lovely path it is. You've been quite fortunate."

"I didn't expect you to know anything about them."

"Oh, I see." His eyes twinkled. "You thought I associated only with Christians and Buddhists. Yes?"

I was thrilled. I wanted to scream, *Thank you, God, thank you, thank you!* Once again, the two strands of my life had crossed and merged. Father Keating and Pir Vilayat even looked alike, both of them tall, thin, with aristocratic features and piercing eyes; both soft-spoken, with a presence that was otherworldly and, at the same time, grounded in the here-and-now. Thomas wore priestly black trousers and sweater, while Pir wore the traditional white Sufi robe that matched his white beard, but I discovered they had one other thing in common: when I talked with them, both made me feel as if I were the most important person in the world.

"Thomas," I said now, gathering my thoughts, "I've been on the spiritual path for a long time. But I can't really believe that God loves me. I have times when I can't rid myself of the thought that somehow I'm bad, and that's why God can't love me. I don't understand how I'm bad, but when this feeling is with me, I have little peace. I know God is love and that these feelings aren't true, that they have to do with my psychological makeup. But I'm tormented by them, some times more than others."

His stared ahead as if he were someplace else, and then his gaze turned toward me, his eyes filled with compassion. "In a way, you've answered your own question. These feelings are always a result of the self-image we cultivated when we were very young. What you mentioned is a common enough problem, but one that is also extremely painful."

I sighed. "I've been in therapy for years, gone on endless retreats—and still, this feeling persists. Perhaps I'm experiencing dark nights of the soul—but I feel I'm going to be punished!" I tried to hold back the tears but couldn't.

He nodded. "Yes, I understand. But *you* must understand that you are not your feelings. Neither are you your thoughts—or your emotions or even who you think you are."

I hesitated, then burst out, "Forgive me, Thomas, but knowing this doesn't help."

He gave a breath of laughter. "No, I suppose it doesn't. Telling oneself anything doesn't help. Obviously, you've worked on yourself for a long time. This is more than most people do. Keep trying to understand how you acquired this image of not being lovable, and then ask God for help in letting it go. This letting go is the same as we do in centering prayer. Centering prayer gives us practice, helps us form a habit of letting go. When all is said and done, we have no choice but to let go in life, again and again, until the final letting go in death—and perhaps even after death." He looked away for a moment. The room's silence was deep and peaceful. Then he said, "It is not just the good things, the things we value, that we must let go. We must also let go of the things that torment us. We do not repress them or deny them, though. We do not struggle with them, using self-discipline. We accept the fact of whatever is in our consciousness—and then we release it."

I remembered Rumi's guesthouse metaphor. Was this the same idea, expressed in different language?

"Everything must be surrendered," Thomas continued. "You may find you even have to let go of God. When you do, you allow the Mystery to be what it is, rather than what you expect or want."

Silence filled the small room for a long moment. Then he said, "What you're tormenting yourself about is a mirage. Everything is a mirage, because we have all we need, and because we have already arrived. Being human, we're not conscious of this, but this is the ultimate truth."

He started to get to his feet, but then he sat down again and said, "When you pray, reverse the process. What I mean by this is that each time you realize you desperately want God, know that God is desperately wanting you. Each time you feel the need to call to God, know that it's God calling out to you. Each time you sense love for the Mystery, know that it's because this Mystery is loving you, passionately, intensely, infinitely. In a way we're incapable of understanding, this God of ours needs us. I can say no more, because words are limiting. They make implications that aren't accurate. They're not nuanced enough for us to grasp what this means. These are things we know only with our heart."

He stood up, and I knew the session was over. I rose to leave, but I had an urge to touch him first. Summoning my courage, I hugged him. His arms hugged me back.

✳✳✳

I gathered much of value from Thomas during those twenty-one days, but what cut through my heart were his words on the last day: "God asks but one thing from us—our permission to allow Him to love us."

I desperately wanted to absorb these words as a living truth that would nourish and sustain me for the rest of my life. Oh, how I wanted this! But my old skepticism emerged instead: *How does Thomas know this?*

This is a kind of metaphor for God's love, that's all. It's not fact!

The God Thomas showed me was too vulnerable. This image of the Divine was so far from the one I had grown up with. The Sufis might have been at home with a God of absolute, unconditional, intimate, and humble love—but I still wasn't. I kept thinking, *God is not supposed to be like this!*

My old image of God was at least one I could rail against. I was like some long-ago woman who worshipped a stone idol. I loved that idol. I loved raging at it, shaking my fist at its stony face. That face was as familiar as my parents'. How could I let it go—and open myself to this terrifying and mysterious replacement? What would happen to me if I did?

Thomas had suggested I also take a closer look at my sense of myself. "See anything familiar there?" he queried gently. "Have you confused God's nature with your own self-image?"

Now, in spite of myself, I continued to ponder his question. Had my self-image shaped my image of God? If I believed I was unlovable, how could I accept Divine love? How could I enter into a relationship with the vulnerable Mystery Father Keating insisted was the foundation of the Universe?

How could I even believe it was real?

As a child, I had felt unloved by my parents, and that experience had shaped my expectations of every relationship since. Even as an adult, I felt suspicious that friends always had an angle. As for my relationships with men, obviously, I told myself, they all had ulterior motives. People might be attracted to my exterior—but at the back of my mind, I always believed that sooner or later everyone would find out I'm not as good as I look.

And so in the days after that first retreat with Thomas, I concluded that I couldn't trust his ideas about God. After all, he too must have an angle, some reason for needing to convince people that his ideas were fact. Obviously, God did not need our permission to be loved, because then God wouldn't be God. I felt very smug, very confident of my theology.

And yet Father Keating's words haunted me. A God who respects us enough to endure rejection? A Divine Sweetness who chooses to lovingly create us with each breath? Love that is truly, infinitely unconditional and vulnerable?

The questions became the background of all my thoughts. I had no answers to them, but I could not dismiss them. Now, years later, I believe the answers are not as important as we might think. Instead, as we open ourselves to the questions themselves, something begins to change within us. Unseen, unconscious, something is transformed. It's like the Jesus Prayer, the simple sentence that when repeated over and over for a lifetime has changed the spiritual and psychological lives of so many people down through the centuries.

The twelfth-century Sufi mystic Ibn Arabi prayed, "Oh Lord, nourish me not with love but with the desire for love." Desire and longing do not seem like nourishment—just the opposite in fact—and yet it was my need that had driven me inward and onward throughout my entire life. And now, in the weeks and the months after the retreat, that need felt as though it were being sharpened, focused, condensed down to a sharper point. Rainer Maria Rilke wrote, "Be patient toward all that is unsolved in your heart and try to love the questions themselves. . . . Live the questions now. Perhaps you will then gradually, without noticing it, live along some distant day into the answer." Looking back, I believe that was the process I had begun.

✳✳✳

There were other retreats with Thomas. Indeed, each year for five years, I attended these twenty-one day retreats. Thomas once said I was addicted to them. I suppose I was addicted to him, or more to the point, what he had to say about God. Grounded in Christianity's mystical tradition, he gave me a new view of Christianity that created a bridge between my Sufi background and my growing love for Christ. Moreover, as I practiced centering prayer, I felt that a deep, unconscious healing was taking place inside me, as though some sort of Divine psychotherapy was going on. As Thomas said, "Psychotherapy is what God has been secretly doing for centuries by other names; that is, he searches through our personal history and heals what needs to be healed, the wounds of childhood or our own self-inflicted wounds."

At last, however, the time came for me to say goodbye to Thomas Keating. On the morning of the final retreat, we gathered around him. Each of us hugged him, a few cried, and when it was my turn, I said to him, "It really hurts to see you go. What do we do now?"

"You have everything in you that I have," he told me. "Look within yourself."

What did I have in me? I thought about that question as I drove back home. One way to discover the answer to that question, I realized, was to use my own "voice"—my creative powers. As I did so, would my own voice begin to teach me?

I made up my mind: the time had come to seek new creative outlets. I could no longer let fear silence me. After all, my name was Bahri!

24

You carry secret treasures.
Didn't you know that?
Rumi

A year earlier I had attended a workshop designed for those who wanted to become presenters for Contemplative Outreach. During the workshop, I'd met a man who conducted a prison ministry in Texas.

Secretly, I had always been drawn to prison ministry, but my life had never led me in that direction. As I talked with the man one afternoon, I confessed my interest in his ministry.

"You could work with women inmates," he told me.

I shook my head. "No, somehow, I always pictured myself with male inmates. I don't know why."

"Well, that's pretty unrealistic," he said bluntly. But then he added, "One thing is lacking in my ministry with the men, though. I don't know how to teach them centering prayer. They need something to guide them, something to encourage them. I'm thinking of writing a workbook—but I don't know how to communicate the nuances of the prayer in words they'll understand. How can I tell them what it means to pray like this, when most of these men don't even pray at all? They need to be persuaded that this form of prayer could do them real good, practical good. As sure as I'm sitting here, I know centering prayer would be the answer to the deep emptiness these men feel."

I hesitated, and then I blurted, "Would you trust me to help you?"

He raised an eyebrow. "Can you write?"

"A little."

He looked thoughtful. "But you don't know these men. You haven't had the experience. You don't know what goes on in their heads. You can't understand their fears, their defensiveness. Their out-and-out cruelty."

"No," I said, "but I do know what it's like to feel imprisoned."

He fell silent then. While I waited for him to speak, I wished I could make him understand that I knew what it meant to have my voice silenced. I wanted to tell him that prisoners must surely have lost their real voices somewhere along the line. They had replaced that deep, true voice with a mini-voice, something small and false to feed their egos, to deceive and boast. How was that any different from what I had done?

I sensed that a practice like centering prayer would, over time, allow these men to experience a dimension of themselves they had never before touched. It would give them refuge, a place of freedom and spaciousness even within the prison walls. And I believed that as much as any hardened criminal, I knew what it was like to face the dark shadows within my own being. This, I was convinced, was a chance to use my true voice.

And so he and I began work together. He provided the study questions and projects, while I wrote about the prayer itself and the freedom it could bring. We titled the book *Pathway to Freedom.*

Before it was published, we sent a copy to Thomas Keating for his approval. He encouraged us to have it published as soon as possible. A few months after publication, it was translated into Spanish, and it is now used in prisons in the United States, Canada, South America, and Mexico.

Co-authoring this book proved to be one of the most profound experiences of my life. Expecting difficulty, I was astonished to see how writing for prisoners came so easily. I felt as though I knew the men who would read the book, as though they and I were somehow united in a common experience. The book wrote itself. As I worked on it, perhaps I was teaching myself as much as I was my intended readers.

Writing this book was sheer delight. It was one of God's secret surprises, a totally unexpected way for me to pursue a ministry that had always called me.

✳✳✳

Meanwhile, during this period of my life, the Crohn's disease that had plagued me most of my life was sapping more and more of my strength. I had less energy now for attending retreats or running around town to give centering prayer workshops. At the same time, I found myself wanting more time to be quiet and alone.

And yet in my solitude, I still wanted to find a way to "sing," to let my creative voice be heard. For so much of my life, I had focused on academic study and intellectual thought, but now I wanted to use the intuitive right side of my brain. Alone in my sunlit room, I played with watercolors, painting flowers, fairies, faces. I had little technical ability, and yet I loved the color, the shapes.

When I confided my frustration with my limitations to an artist friend, she suggested that I try something new. "You might like writing icons," she said. "It's so stylized, you don't need any drawing ability." Icon writing, my friend told me, had more to do with prayer than artistic talent. "You trace the figures," she said. "The rest is easy."

Her words convinced me to give icons a try. But she was wrong. It wasn't easy.

I began working with the wife of a Russian Orthodox pastor who taught icon writing based on the Russian Byzantine tradition that dates back to the sixth century. I had always romanticized the monks of old, thinking I would have enjoyed their lifestyle (though in reality, I would probably not have done well at all without hot showers and a warm house), so I was immediately enchanted.

The word "writing" as opposed to "painting" is used in iconography to set off this activity from the usual sort of artistic painting. My teacher told me that God guides the iconographer's hand; each brushstroke is a form of meditation. Before beginning a new icon, I spent time in prayer. And then once I had begun, I had to be careful to dwell in a state of inner peace. As I worked, I noticed that each time I allowed a negative thought to linger in my mind, I made a mistake with my brush.

At first, I had no sense of the sacred as I worked at this new activity. I was too intent on choosing the right colors, mastering various techniques, placing the gold properly, and, above all, learning how to write faces that expressed a tender divinity. I kept forgetting I had to be at peace within myself, rather than compete with myself. My perfectionism stuck its pointy nose in my back, nudging at me. Meanwhile, my teacher's Ukranian accent sometimes hindered my understanding when she wanted to communicate something important to me. Often I became frustrated. I was tempted to throw up my hands and quit.

One day, after several months of instruction, my teacher said to me, "Why you want to write icon?"

Startled by her question, especially so late in the game, I responded, "Because I think they're beautiful."

She shook her head. "Not enough good reason. You need to want to pray. You need to want see what is beauty before you make it."

I was a little peeved. I'd been working so hard, after all. "I don't understand," I said.

"Icon not an art object. The icon a window, not a picture. You look at icon to see *greater* beauty."

I looked around her studio. "What could be more beautiful than these? I want to learn how to create this beauty. As you do. What's wrong with that?"

She shook her head again. "I don't create beauty. God create beauty when you look *into* icon. Not *at* icon."

"Into the icon?" I repeated.

"Yes. Like through window."

I looked at one of her icons, a beautiful portrait of Mary in gold and blue. "How can that be a window?" I asked. "It's beautiful . . . but it is what it is."

She let out an impatient breath. "Ah, you are like child, not understand, because you no want to."

"No, please," I answered. "I'm trying to understand what you want to tell me, but— Oh, never mind. Let's try again. What window are you talking about?"

"Window of soul. You look at eyes on Mother of God, and she not just looking back. She show you more; she show you window into heaven, and when you learn to see, then she talk to you too."

I stared at her, and her words slowly took on meaning. Until then, I hadn't grasped what writing an icon really meant. For me it had been a peaceful sort of artistic endeavor. I loved the beauty of the icons, but now I saw that the icon was a vehicle for an exchange between the spiritual and the physical realms. I went back to my work with a new understanding.

Writing icons is a long, slow, process. You are never sure of the outcome as you work. Each time I felt I had gained control, almost instantly I was proven wrong. And when I did write well, I was surprised at myself. The icon I had written was somehow separate from me, rather than anything for which I could take credit.

The icons, I came to believe, expressed Something that longed to be expressed. Writing them was like singing, back in the days when I was a child. During this quiet phase of my life, I sensed the past flowing into the present, the present reaching backward into the past.

On Christmas morning that year, I found myself thinking about Blanchefleur. I knew she had moved to California, but we had not been in touch for years. On impulse, I picked up the phone and dialed her number.

We exchanged the usual pleasantries about our families and mutual friends. And then I asked her, "Are you still a Sufi?"

"Yes," she said. "My husband and I go back to the Abode once a year to conduct retreats there. But, Bahri, I'm also following the Diamond Approach."

I had to confess my ignorance. She explained that it was a path of spiritual transformation that combined modern psychology with specific practices.

I wanted to know more, of course. Most of all, though, I didn't want to lose my connection to Blanchefleur again. Twenty years before, she had been my connection to myself and to God. Now, after all these years, I had found her again.

"It's not like the Sufi spiritual guidance I used to give you years ago," she warned me. "It's a different approach altogether, and it employs more psychology than what we did together back then."

She was in the midst of a seven-year program, I learned. When she had completed it, she would be ordained by the Ridhwan School.

"So, it's another spiritual path?" I asked her. "Different from Sufism?"

"Yes," she said. "Different in that Sufism is an ancient path, while this path combines spiritual insights with the psychological developments of the past century."

"Like psychotherapy then?"

"No," she answered patiently, "it is not psychotherapy per se. It is a path to our fullest potential. It provides a precise method for inner work, using modern psychological methods—focusing, questioning, interpretation—but the goal is the transformation of the soul."

"But how did this start? Who started it?"

"It's based on the teachings of Hameed Ali, who writes under the pen name, A. H. Almaas. He's from Kuwait, but when he was eighteen, he moved to California to attend the University of California in Berkeley. While working on his Ph.D. in physics, he reached a turning point that led him to inquire into the psychological and spiritual aspects of human nature. What resulted was the development of a teaching that integrated the mystical teachings of many traditions—Sufism, Buddhism, as well as depth psychology, and his own mystical revelations."

My life had come full circle again. I was certain that God had arranged that my path would cross Blanchefleur's once more, just as God had brought Bill and me back together after being apart from one another for half a lifetime. Now, despite the three thousand miles that separated us, I was reconnecting with Blanchefleur.

***

I had hoped to regain the personal relationship we had once had, the sense of friendship. I would have loved to know Blanchefleur's thoughts and desires, I wanted news of her family and her life—but that didn't happen. When we spoke on the phone, my sense of the personal Blanchefleur was gone. Our conversations were empty of everything except the challenge to confront myself and God.

The relationship between a spiritual teacher and a seeker is not one that we've often cultivated in the West. When we do look for spiritual direction, many times we expect to be instructed, the way we were in school. The East, however, sees the teacher's role differently. The spiritual teacher brings about the student's recognition of her own pre-existing nature, rather than an understanding of some new body of knowledge. The Western idea is that the student will "know more" when the teaching is completed, while the Eastern idea is that the teacher points to something that is already present in the student.

As Westerners, we've also come to expect that, at some level, the purpose of all social interactions is to stroke our egos. Consequently, we tend to expect our teachers to offer us the love and support we get from our close friends. Blanchefleur made clear, however, that this was not the nature of our new relationship. I began to understand a little better one day as I was reading a book titled *Fragments of a Love Story* by a Sufi sheik named Llewellyn Vaughan-Lee. "The teacher," wrote Vaughan-Lee, "is in essence an empty space through which the energy of the Divine can nourish the disciple, or become a mirror that simply reflects the disciple's true self. . . . [and] what is most precious within a human being: the desire for Truth and the ability to live this desire—the potential to go Home."

In the months that followed, Blanchefleur offered me that empty space where I could discover both my true self and the Beloved. I spoke with her each week for an hour, and during that time, we engaged in what the Diamond Approach refers to as Inquiry, the principle practice of this path. During these times of Inquiry, Blanchefleur encouraged me to be conscious of feelings, thoughts, energy, and all my physical faculties and sensations. The goal was to discover the Essence of my own being, grounded in the present moment.

In *Being and the Meaning of Life*, Almsas wrote:

> *Ideas and experiences from the past, from early childhood as well as later on, good and bad, form the foundation of your assumptions about who you are. Your mind holds on to these childhood happenings and stores them in its memory. They*

become the building blocks of what you think
you are. . . . What understanding gives us is the
possibility of actually seeing through this process.
Without understanding, you'll just identify with
these old self-images.

The Diamond Approach made me think of the line
from T. S. Eliot: "We shall not cease from exploration,
and the end of all our exploring will be to arrive where
we started and know the place for the first time."

All my life, I had pursued God with my mind, relating
to spirituality as though it were an academic inquiry, an
intellectual problem that could be solved with enough
thought. I had begun to use my creativity as another way
to engage with the spiritual life, and now Blanchefleur
was teaching me to use my body as the door into what
she called Being.

And just as I began to listen to my body, the messages
it was sending me turned into a scream. My Crohn's disease was no longer content to lurk in the background of
my life. Suddenly, it had become life threatening.

25

Really, everything and everyone is a shadow of the Beloved,
and our seeking is His seeking,
our words are His words. . . .
We spend our lives searching everywhere for Him,
while all the time, we're looking straight at Him.
Sitting right next to Him, we keep asking,
"Oh Beloved, where is the Beloved?"
Rumi

I hadn't realized I was so sick. I thought I was just tired.
So when my doctor examined me and said, "I'm calling
an ambulance to take you to the hospital," I was taken by
surprise, to say the least.

But I also felt relieved. I was tired of my Crohn's. I
was tired of being tired. Maybe finally something would
"fix it."

On the ride to the hospital, a young paramedic told
me about his family. I hardly listened. I was just too
tired, so overwhelmed with weariness that all I wanted
was a bed.

At the hospital, I was so grateful to be lying down
and stationary that I dozed through my CAT scan.
Dimly, I watched as doctor after doctor looked at the

scan. They all shook their heads at what they saw, but I didn't much care. "You need surgery," the doctors said. "Immediately."

Fine, I thought. *Just let me sleep.*

***

A day and a half later, I awoke in a hospital bed. An intern told me I had undergone major surgery. I had no memory of it.

But I did have a very sharp memory of something else. I remembered lying on a hospital stretcher, while nurses hovered over me. They each had black, black eyes, as black as inkblots against their white uniforms, black as holes in the hospital's white walls, black as nails that hammered my body to the stretcher. Terrified, I struggled to get up, but one after another, the nurses pushed me back. Their eyes flashed in sync, I realized, as though they were actually one entity.

I wanted Bill. I screamed his name.

"He's not coming," they said, one after another. "He's never coming. And even if he did, we wouldn't let him in."

One of them shut the door and bolted it. "There," she said.

"If he tries to get in," said another, "we might let him in."

"Or," said another nurse, "we might kill him."

I screamed Bill's name again, but they screamed back at me even louder. "We could kill him. We could let him in, and you wouldn't even know the difference. We could kill him, we could kill him, we could kill him. . ."

I couldn't scream anymore. They were harpies, medusas, gorgons. They had turned me to stone—and a stone has no voice.

✳✳✳

This was the only memory I had of the time after I came to the hospital. It didn't feel like a dream. It felt real.

As I lay there, trying to remember, I noticed a vase of flowers on the stand beside my bed. The card told me that my daughters had sent them to me. I fixed my eyes on the blossoms and drifted back to sleep.

When I opened my eyes again, I saw a pietà on the stand next to the flowers. I squinted at it, trying to make sense of what I was seeing. There was something odd about the small statue.

Instead of Mary holding the body of Jesus, I realized, this pietà showed Jesus holding the body of a woman. I blinked, but it was still there. Still looking at it, I fell asleep yet again.

When I woke the next time, there was no pietà on the stand, only the vase of flowers. I lay on the hospital bed feeling puzzled—and full of a quiet joy.

The joy continued through the ten days I was in the hospital. The nurses—perfectly kind women with quite normal eyes—were surprised by my calm reaction when I discovered I had lost my entire colon. I was down to eighty-seven pounds, weak and shaky—and yet at the same time, I felt energized, filled with a new sense of life flowing through my body.

A quiet awareness grew inside me as each day passed: I was the woman who lay in Jesus' lap.

I couldn't tell anyone. It was a hallucination, after all, brought on by anesthesia and painkillers.

But what did it mean? Smiling to myself, I pondered the question.

I went home and began my long convalescence. On the one hand, I was quite sure the "vision" was merely the trick of a drugged brain. And on the other hand? I was simply happy, totally and utterly. For the first time, I truly knew I was loved.

I decided to write to a woman who had worked with Thomas Keating, Cynthia Bourgeault. She is an Episcopal priest, an author, and a spiritual teacher. I described my experience to her—and almost immediately I received her response: "It seems that your encounter with those hellish figures and the safe passage through was a mini Harrowing of Hell experience, and you have come out the other end of it upheld by your own force infused with something greater. Draw on that strength and go deeper."

A few months later, I attended Cynthia's Wisdom School and spoke with her in person. She again assured me that the experience had been "real."

"Be grateful," she told me.

Years later, I'm still searching for what it all meant. I believe, though, that this experience was the turning point in my life, the climax of my old story. From here on, I'm in new territory. In some real way, Jesus lifted me in his arms and took me away from the past, from my old ideas about myself, the old judgments and fears. I don't know what lies ahead. I'm heading into unfamiliar, uncharted land.

All those years that I had been on a spiritual path, something had been missing. My sense of "me" resided within my brain, while my body remained empty, as if it didn't exist. Now, for the first time, I began to understand what Blanchefleur had been trying to teach me, what Thomas Keating and the Sufis and everyone else had tried to get me to see.

The Incarnation is real. God became flesh and lived with us. But it didn't end with Jesus. We embody Divinity. God is revealed not only through our intellects, not even only through what we think of as our hearts, our emotions. The Divine lives in our bodies, these broken, imperfect things that nevertheless are the places where God is revealed to us and through us.

But we are sleeping, unaware. We need life's furious wake-up calls to shatter our oblivion. The most intense and unmerciful call of all is the one that comes to us from death, the threat to these bodies of ours that we otherwise take for granted.

Like most everyone, I fear death. Regardless of what I've learned on the spiritual path, regardless of my belief in the infinite love of God, that existential dread still lingers within me. Even with my new awareness of Divine

love, the old, primal fears are there: the fear of abandonment, rejection, and punishment, all rolled up into the
word "death."

As I've said before, my life isn't a novel. I can't wrap
up the story of my spiritual journey by weaving all the
strands together in a smooth and satisfactory pattern.
After that most spiritual moment of my life—a very real
turning point—the old fears didn't miraculously disappear. To my disappointment, they were still there.

They're part of me. They are my lot in life. They hold
me back on my spiritual path, they drag me down—and
at the same time, they spur me on.

26

God picks up the world's flute and blows into it.
Each note is a need, a passion, a longing, a pain
that arises in our own hearts.
When you feel this wind passing through you,
remember the mouth that blew the breath.
Let your note be clear.
Don't look for a way to end it.
Be your note. . . .
Sing loud!
Rumi

This past year, I ventured into a desert in Southern California with a group of friends. I soon discovered that this was a far different desert from the Sahara that had spoken so to me years ago. Instead of endless wind-scoured sand where only small fleeting blooms took root, this desert was filled with strange plants that thrived wherever they could nestle into the earth.

Our guide, a man named Eller, understood this wilderness. We soon learned that he regarded every stone and grain of sand with a shaman-like clarity. Guiding people through nature's desolate places was more than a job for him. He seemed to know the moods of coyotes and quails, and he spoke the wind's language, deciphering where each movement of air originated and where it was headed. For him, we realized, the Earth was a cherished and living entity.

He asked if we had ever experienced a sweat lodge. Some of us had, some of us hadn't, but we were all eager to have that experience here, where we sensed the sacred all around us.

The next morning, we climbed higher up the mountain, and by midday, we had dug a ditch on the mountainside for the fire. Eller cut wood from green aspen trees to build the frame, and we brought our heaviest, dark-colored blankets to drape over the framework. A couple of us picked up pebbles to create a pathway for transporting the rocks from the fire to the lodge. We made a small stone altar.

When it was done, we went back to our campsite and collapsed in a circle around our guide. He seemed as fresh as when the day began. "Well, I think that's it for today," he said and pulled his cap further down on his forehead. "We'll meet at 3:30 a.m., and then we'll light the fire for the rocks. The sweat will begin at 5 a.m., right after the sun rises over those mountains there." He pointed a finger toward the east.

We climbed into our sleeping bags, but I couldn't sleep. I had experience with sweat lodges, which both comforted me and made me anxious. I reminded myself that as long as I kept myself from focusing on the heat and concentrated on my breath instead, I'd be able to avoid becoming claustrophobic. *Soften your belly*, I reminded myself. *Let go. Surrender.*

The next morning, I crawled out of my sleeping bag to find a sky that was still velvet black and strewn with stars. I stretched, feeling as though I could reach up through the soft darkness and grab one of those silver lights.

As we gathered together, ready for the climb up the mountain to the sweat lodge we'd built, Eller reassured us. "Whenever you wish to leave, you can leave. I want no one to feel unduly uncomfortable. This will be sacred space. You will be surrounded by sacred beings who protect and love us. Anyone who doesn't wish to continue, however, please, simply make the decision to leave. I'll be there to pull up the blankets and let you out."

We set off from our campsite. In the distance, further up the mountain, we saw that the fire was already built, its red and orange light flickering against the darkness. The closer we drew to that fire, the more the flames seemed to take on shapes, like many-colored dancers. Eller had already placed the large stones in the fire, and we waited by the fire for them to heat. The contrast of the fire's bright heat against the morning's soft silence seemed otherworldly somehow, almost surreal. I felt a sense of strangeness, and at the same time, I was intensely present, aware of each sound and scent.

When at last I pulled my gaze away from the fire, I saw that the black sky had faded to gray in the east. Soft light spread over the sky, changing black to bronze, and then pink, gold, and finally an orange so intense that the fire's flames paled by comparison. Morning had arrived.

"It's time," Eller said softly.

We pulled off our outer clothes, leaving only our bathing suits, and gathered around the opening of the lodge. The look Eller gave us was level, assessing, with a hint of compassion. "Remember," he said, "we're going to divide the sweat into three sessions. They'll be a fourth one as well—but that's only for those who are nuts."

A few of us smiled uneasily, but no one laughed. His eyes moved over our faces. "Remember," he continued, "if you decide to cut it short—no shame, no embarrassment, no regrets. Everyone is different—and sweat lodges aren't for everyone. Understand me?"

We nodded and went inside. Eller pulled the blankets over the opening; in total darkness, we took our seats on the ground, while Eller placed the two fired-up rocks in the pit. We heard him pouring water, slowly and gently, one drip at a time, and then the soft hiss as each drop met the hot stone. Soon, steam filled the small space.

The total darkness gave me the sense that I was alone in that hot, wet place. Only the touch of another's skin on each side of me reminded me that we were here together. Eller's voice filled the darkness with a tribal chant, and one by one, we joined him.

But at first, my thoughts wandered. I found myself remembering a recent conversation with Blanchefleur, replaying in my mind the words that had caused me so much pain.

"After a great deal of prayer and thought," she had told me, "I'm now convinced that the Diamond Approach is not for you."

I had argued with her, tried to persuade her she was wrong, but she was firm. "All right," I said at last. "Perhaps it wasn't the path itself but my reconnection to you that was most important to me."

"Yes," she said, "I believe that's closer to the truth."

"But you'll continue to be my teacher? We'll continue our weekly sessions?"

"No," she said. "We won't, Bahri."

I felt nothing at first, only a faint sense of freedom. I knew I couldn't turn to anyone else to give me spiritual direction now. My endless seeking for new insights from yet another wise person, someone who would finally have *the* answer I needed—all that was behind me now. From here on, I'd go it alone. Part of me was simply curious to see what this would be like, walking into the unknown with only God as a guide.

But then, another part of me woke up, like a terrified child who opens her eyes and finds Mommy has suddenly disappeared. The old feelings of rejection, abandonment, and fear swept over me in waves. Between these tides of emotion, I struggled to make sense of what I was feeling, but I couldn't concentrate. Just as I thought I was adjusting to this latest development, another wave slammed into me. I had plunged into a sea of hopelessness and anger.

Each day my anger intensified. Finally, I could stand it no longer. I sat down in my room and attempted to sense the rage in my body, a practice Blanchefleur had drilled into me. The anger deepened and broadened until I felt that each of my muscles had turned into steel—and then something broke inside me. The bands of emotion that had held me rigid snapped, replaced by a sharp pain in my chest. I began to cry.

My heart had broken. The old trite words were the only ones that described what I felt. The shattered pieces were all that was left of all my old hopes and efforts. I had longed for spiritual wisdom and connection to the Divine—but there was nothing left, only sadness and bitter pain.

Now, sitting here in the steamy darkness, the chanting rising around me in waves of sound, words from Rumi came to me: "No cure exists for this pain but to die."

And then my thoughts disappeared, as the chant filled the space, filled my chest and belly, occupied every space in my mind. When, the first session ended, I was surprised. I had barely noticed the passage of time.

One person decided to leave now. We waited five minutes; then Eller threw more hot stones into the pit and drew the blankets across the opening to the outside air.

This time the air was even hotter, the steam thicker. Sweat poured off me. The dark air was something I could reach out and touch with my hand, as though I were inside a thunderhead before a storm. I struggled to breathe.

According to tradition, your life flashes before your eyes as you die. Now, in the darkness, I saw in my mind that frightened Bronx kid mourning for her mother, gazing at the Blessed Virgin with so much hope. I found myself smiling at my teenage self playing truant, sitting in the dark movie theater. My smile faded as I felt in my heart her fear and shame when she lost her voice. The resentment and frustration of my first marriage replaced those emotions—and then I tasted the courage and high hopes with which I had set out on so many spiritual adventures.

And then I fell back into myself, here, now, empty.

Once again, I heard Rumi whispering to me:

> *Praise the emptiness that blanks out existence,*
> *that erases the presence*
> *of everything we thought was real. . . .*
> *Praise to that happening over and over!*
> *For years, I pulled my own existence*
> *out of emptiness.*
> *Now, with one swoop, one swing of the arm,*
> *that work is over.*
> *I am free now.*
> *Free of who I was. . . . Free of fear and hope,*
> *free of the endless wanting*
> *that was like a mountain too steep to ever climb.*

Can I let go of it all, all the wanting? All the beliefs I've clung to, all the values I've held, all the people I love? Can I accept emptiness? Can I become emptiness?

"Die before death," I remembered the Sufis saying, "and resurrect now."

And then, again, Eller's voice filled the small space, sweeping over my thoughts, anchoring me here in *this* moment. This time he was singing, not chanting, and one by one, tentatively at first, the rest of us joined the song. I concentrated on the unfamiliar melody, the strange lyrics, and my heart lightened.

Just as I felt I was getting good at singing the song, the session ended. Two more people left now. Six of us remained.

As Eller closed the opening again, the darkness seemed even deeper, denser, heavier, like ocean waves pounding against me. I struggled to anchor my thoughts on God.

It's always been so easy for me to think about God, I realized, to talk about the Divine. Joyful or sad, angry or elated, God is my favorite subject. Maybe each new realization was just relearning an old lesson—but still, I'd been trying so damn hard all these years to make sense of God! Surely that must count for something?

There in the overpowering dark, though, it occurred to me that effort implies our attention is focused on the future. Living in the present moment holds no effort. No more trying, no more working, no more struggling. Simply being. No more ego.

But how can ego get rid of ego?

And then Rumi was there with me again in the dark, murmuring, "The wave named Am-I-Not-Your-Lord? has broken the container of your body. Now that the container is broken, you'll be able to see. Now you and the Divine will be one."

I felt as if something was rising out of my heart's broken pieces, something bright and innocent, something spontaneous and beyond my control. It was not me letting go through any effort of mine; it was letting-go rising through me, like a partner who leads the dance.

And then the dancers became the dance. No separation. A moment of utter union as I chanted with Eller.

This time, when it was over, each of us left the lodge to breathe some fresh air before the fourth session began. As I returned to the opening of the lodge, I realized that only two others were crazy enough to continue.

I hesitated, not sure I really wanted to go back into the small, dark space. Maybe I had had enough. Before I could make a decision, Eller cried out, "Now or never!" Leaving my mind somewhere outside with the coyotes, I entered for the fourth time.

Each session had been more physically intense than the last. This time, the steam, heat, and sweat crossed some line, beyond intense, into a sensation that seemed unbearable. I thought I might truly die.

I touched my heaving chest with my hand, and I felt a moment's fondness for this body that has served me so well. It has carried me through tragedy and joy, a good

and faithful servant. To say good-bye to it would be sad—
but in that moment, death seemed like a gracious escort,
holding out a gentle hand to lead me into something
greater. "Death is our wedding with Eternity," Rumi said.

"Now I lay me down to sleep," I found myself whispering in response, "I pray the Lord my soul to keep. If I
should die before I wake, I pray the Lord my soul to take."

The words of the old childhood prayer, my earliest
connection to God, were like the anchoring knot in the
long strand of my life. The little girl who prayed them was
still there with me in the darkness. So was the rebellious
teenager, the scared young wife and mother, the hopeful
woman who set off for the Refuge. Their voices were the
only voice I had, I realized. It was their pain, their broken
hearts, that had called to me through the years.

And what had called to them?

Panting and sweating, I pondered the question. Long
ago, Gertrud, my Jungian therapist, had taught me that
the Self is also the Divine, that God's voice was my
own—but although I had grasped at the idea, I had never
truly brought it inside my heart. The Sufis had taught me
that God says to us, "I was a Hidden Treasure, and I loved
to be known—so I created you." I found myself remembering another Sufi saying: "God cut Himself off from His
own light in order that we might grow."

And then the answer came to me, clear and sweet:
Inside my own heart, the still, small Voice had always
spoken. This wasn't an all-powerful and mighty God, but
a vulnerable God who had loved me enough to go with

me into the darkness, to suffer with me through each moment of my life. His voice was the treasure buried in my heart. He was the child calling to me, the adolescent girl, the young woman. All along, it had been God.

In the midst of these thoughts, I heard Eller say, "This time I want you to make your own sounds. I want you to use your voice any way you want. Don't be afraid of using any sound that comes up, that emerges from your belly, your chest, your throat. Whatever it is, scream it out as loud as you can. Don't think about what you're doing. Forget about yourself. Be only your voice. Don't listen to any voice but your own."

I was past the ability to think about what I was doing now. All my thoughts had disappeared, melted into the wet, black air. The analytical, skeptical part of me was too sodden with heat to even raise an eyebrow. Panting, struggling to stay calm within the experience, I forced myself to do what Eller asked. I opened my mouth. I called on my vocal cords to make noise.

And then, in the darkness, I heard a voice I had never heard before. It wasn't a singing voice, or an animal voice, nor was it even really a human voice. It filled the steam, it burst through the heat. At the same time, I felt something pushing through me, something strong and primitive, like a tornado or an avalanche or a buffalo stampede. And all the while, the song continued, growing more and more powerful.

At last, I realized it was coming from my own throat. Its vibration filled every cavity of my body as it poured into the dark space, filling the steam with its strange melody. It was my voice—and yet not mine. Utterly unknown, and yet deeply familiar.

This was the voice that had called to me for so long.

My Song.

MARIETTA BAHRI DELLA PENNA

The minute I heard my first love story,
I started looking for you,
not knowing how blind I was being.
Turns out, lovers don't finally meet somewhere.
They're in each other all along.
Rumi

See? I was watching over you the whole time,
wherever you went,
so that I could bring you back to this land.
Genesis 28:15

**Touching God:
Experiencing Metaphors
for the Divine**
Author: Ellyn Sanna
Price: $12.95
Paperback
Ebook Available
160 pages
ISBN: 978-1-933630-93-9

This is a gentle invitation to an experience of God that is immediate and intimate. Drawing from both her own life and a range of sources, Ellyn Sanna shows how the lived symbol is often more truly felt than the theology behind it. A profound awareness of this helps us counter a cold, abstract image of God and make all of life sacramental. Beautifully written, *Touching God* uses readily grasped symbols for God found in the natural world, such as wind, water, darkness, light, rock, bread, and more. It includes human roles as metaphor, showing God as gardener, housewife, host, child, friend, lover, spouse, and self. It complements the lovely text with quotes from scripture, as well as classic and contemporary spiritual writers. This book is both very personal yet universally embracing while it helps readers find an image of God that speaks to their own deepest experience.

Jesus and Lao Tzu:
Adventures with
the Tao Te Ching

Author: George Breed

Price: $14.95

Paperback

Ebook Available

238 pages

ISBN: 978-1-62524-107-8

"*How can I describe this book? If I say it is brilliant, crazy, hilarious, sobering, vulgar, and sublime, all those words are true-but they are certainly not enough to express the contents of Jesus & Lao Tzu. The book defies being categorized or neatly summarized. It will have to suffice if I say simply this: the book's words make me happier, freer, and wiser. If you read it with an open heart, I predict it will do the same for you.*"

—Kenneth McIntosh, author of *Water from an Ancient Well: Celtic Spirituality for Modern Life.*

Brother Lawrence:
A Christian Zen Master

Author: Anamchara Books

Price: $12.95

Paperback

Ebook Available

104 pages

ISBN: 978-1-933630-97-7

The winter I was eighteen, I stood looking at the bare branches of a tree. . . . My awareness was suddenly opened, so that I saw God.

This is the beginning of Brother Lawrence's spiritual journey, a journey that made him stand out to the Christian community of his day (he lived c. 1614-1691), not because he was a great thinker, a gifted speaker, or a talented writer—but simply because of the way he lived his life.

This way of life echoes the teachings of Zen. Surrender yourself to God and you will be equally at peace in both suffering and joy, Brother Lawrence told one of his visitors. When a person does not cling, wrote the Buddha centuries earlier, she is not agitated.

Anamchara Books
Books to Inspire
Your Spiritual Journey

In Celtic Christianity, an *anamchara* is a soul friend, a companion and mentor (often across the miles and the years) on the spiritual journey. Soul friendship entails a commitment to both accept and challenge, to reach across all divisions in a search for the wisdom and truth at the heart of our lives.

At Anamchara Books, we are committed to creating a community of soul friends by publishing books that lead us into deeper relationships with God, the Earth, and each other. These books connect us with the great mystics of the past, as well as with more modern spiritual thinkers. They are designed to build bridges, shaping an inclusive spirituality where we all can grow.

To find out more about Anamchara Books and order our books, visit **www.AnamcharaBooks.com** today.

Anamchara Books
Vestal, New York 13850
www.AnamcharaBooks.com

Made in the USA
Las Vegas, NV
26 September 2021